WHERE'S MY DINNER?

Where's My Dinner?

REAL RECIPES
FOR BUSY PEOPLE
from
The Daily Telegraph

MOYRA FRASER

JOHN MURRAY

Illustrations by Louise Morgan

Text © Moyra Fraser 1998, 1999, 2000 and 2003

First published in 2003 by John Murray (Publishers)
A division of Hodder Headline

A CIP catalogue record for this title is available
from the British Library

ISBN 0-7195-5526-4

Typeset in 11.5/14pt Bembo

Printed and bound in Great Britain by
Clays Ltd, St Ives plc

John Murray (Publishers)
338 Euston Road London NW1 3BH

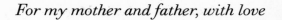

For my mother and father, with love

CONTENTS

Introduction   ix

1. Fish and Shellfish   1

2. Chicken and Game   29

3. Meat   61

4. Pasta and Risotto   119

5. Eggs, Bacon, Pastries, Potatoes etc!   149

6. Served with . . .   179

Index   193

INTRODUCTION

Cooking has taken on a new dimension for me now that I am married with a young family. As a single girl on *Good Housekeeping* magazine I cooked and ate my way through dozens of dishes every day knowing I could return home at night to a big bowl of salad or some fresh fruit and no one to say 'where's my dinner?' Now, happily with more than just myself to think about, I know just what a juggling act life can be and how the daily task of providing something good for supper, that is, something that hasn't come ready-made from the supermarket or take-away, can become a chore. But it needn't. My philosophy now is 'keep it simple'. Try and buy the best ingredients you can and then do as little as possible to them. After all it's only a tasty supper we're preparing, not striving for a Michelin star. From Monday to Friday most of us just want fuss-free food, nothing pretentious and certainly nothing with more than about eight ingredients (and most of those I want to find in the cupboard or fridge). Quite often it's just a good idea for a different seasoning or accompaniment that we're looking for and not a full-blown recipe.

So when I was asked to write a column for the Saturday *Telegraph* I knew exactly the recipes and ideas I wanted to share – it was the simple but delicious ones that made life easy for me and didn't turn cooking the evening meal into a palaver.

This book collects the best of the column's recipes with dozens of new ones. Most of the dishes are cooked and ready in half an hour, while some others take ten minutes to prepare and an hour or so left to simmer in the oven. I love those too as it leaves me time to do something else or put my feet up with a glass of wine.

And although I hope you try the recipes as I like them here, I also hope you'll then twiddle and tweak them to your own taste – add more garlic or leave it out altogether, use a different herb or try extra lemon juice. Please don't think that you have to follow them too rigidly. I'm sure you'll find many that will become firm favourites. Most of the recipes are for two but they are certainly good enough and easy enough to double up if you want to share them with friends.

CHAPTER 1

Fish and Shellfish

Skate with Hot Tomato Salsa
Serves 2

A big-flavoured, garlicky salsa is such a brilliant accompaniment to any pan-fried or grilled fish. I particularly love it with skate but try it with swordfish and tuna too. If you enjoy a bit of heat then add a larger pinch of chilli flakes to the salsa.

2 skate wings, skinned, about 700g/1½lb in weight
salt and freshly ground black pepper
1 tablespoon plain flour
olive oil

For the Salsa
about 125g/4oz really ripe tomatoes
1 tablespoon capers, drained and rinsed in cold water
½ red onion, finely chopped
a generous handful of flat leaf parsley, roughly chopped
a small pinch dried chilli flakes
balsamic vinegar

Mix together all the ingredients for the salsa except the balsamic vinegar with a good drizzle of olive oil. Taste and add plenty of seasoning. Lightly coat the skate in seasoned flour then heat about two tablespoons of oil in a large frying pan. Add the fish and fry until golden. It should be done in three or four minutes. Lift it out onto warm plates then wipe out the pan and add the salsa mixture. Stir over the heat for about 1 minute then add about a tablespoon of balsamic vinegar. Spoon the hot salsa over the fish and eat straight away.

Roast Cod with Lime and Chilli
Serves 2

Cod is regularly on my shopping list, especially the thick fillet or 'loin' for roasting. I always buy it with the skin still on as this forms a crisp crust that keeps the cod's fat flakes moist and juicy underneath. This is an absurdly easy supper and quick to cook. I've left the quantity of chilli vague. If you can take it fiery, use about half a small chilli. If not, use the equivalent of a small pinch. When squeezing the lime, I find that it's easier if it's cut into wedges rather than simply cut in half.

While the cod is cooking there should be just enough time to boil some sweet potatoes (the orange-fleshed variety) just like ordinary potatoes but add a peeled clove of garlic to the bubbling water. When the potatoes are tender mash them with the garlic and plenty of butter. Serve the cod on a mound of the mash with some extra lime to squeeze on top. If you want to make it look smarter to serve to friends add a handful of coriander leaves just before serving.

> 2 thick pieces cod fillet or loin, about 200g/7oz each, with
>   skin
> salt and freshly ground black pepper
> grated rind and juice of 1 lime
> some red chilli, seeded and finely chopped
> small pinch ground allspice
> 1 tablespoon light soft brown sugar
> 2 teaspoons light soy sauce
> olive oil

Preheat the oven to 220C/425F/gas mark 7. Season the cod fillets then stir together all the other ingredients, except the oil. The mixture should be both sweet and sour so add a pinch more sugar if you think it too sharp.

Drizzle a little olive oil over the base of a small, ovenproof frying pan or roasting tin just large enough to hold the fish. Heat the oil on the hob and when it starts to shimmer put the fish, skin side down, into the pan. Leave it to cook over a brisk heat until the skin has turned golden and started to crisp. This will only take a minute. Spoon on the lime and chilli mixture, turn the fish over and transfer to the oven. Roast for about 7–10 minutes depending upon the thickness of the fish. The flakes should be opaque and separate easily. Eat straight away with some Sizzling Greens, see page 181.

A Quick Fish Pie
Serves 2

This is a cracker of a recipe. It's both simple and yet big on flavour. It's a much reduced version of the more time-consuming traditional pie where the fish is poached and a sauce is made but it does rely on a little care being taken with the ingredients.

Try to get the freshest smoked haddock or cod you can find. The ready-wrapped supermarket fillets in their polystyrene trays always look a little too dry and sad for my liking. I've got to confess to fond childhood memories of 'yellow fish' bought shining and fresh from the fish van that came to our gate from Arbroath each week but now I do buy the un-dyed smoked fillets.

Don't skimp on the parsley. Fresh parsley is an essential addition; its bright, clean taste lifts the smoky richness of the fish. A good quality crème fraîche is also essential. They're not all the same and to my mind the thick, gently acidic Crème Fraîche d'Isigny is the best you can buy.

The cooked fish in its garlicky cooking liquor is a meal in itself if spooned into old-fashioned soup plates and eaten with some crusty bread, or served with some nutty brown rice and spinach.

4 or 5 large floury potatoes, preferably Maris Pipers or
    Desirée, peeled and roughly chopped
salt and freshly ground black pepper
1 medium-sized fillet smoked cod or haddock, about
    350g/12oz
palmful chopped fresh parsley
2 garlic cloves, crushed or sliced
about 50g/2oz unsalted butter
olive oil
1 teaspoon Dijon mustard
200ml tub or carton crème fraîche

Put the potatoes into a large pan of cold water with a good seasoning of salt and bring up to the boil. Cover with a lid, reduce the heat and simmer for about 20 minutes or until they are very tender.

While the potatoes are cooking cut the fish into large pieces, bigger than bite-sized, and put them into a bowl with the parsley and garlic (I usually do this with my kitchen scissors straight into the bowl to save the hassle of scrubbing the chopping board afterwards). Stir the fish gently to coat in the garlicky mixture.

Heat half the butter in a frying pan with a drizzle of olive oil until it starts to foam and sizzle. Drop the fish pieces into the pan and leave them to fry over a high heat for about 1 minute to allow them to form a golden crust on the underside. Turn over and fry the other side. This shouldn't take longer than 2–3 minutes or the fish will over-cook.

Take the pan off the heat; add the mustard then spoon dollops of the crème fraîche into the fish. Leave it to melt in the heat of the pan without stirring to prevent the fish from breaking up then spoon the mixture into a small ovenproof dish. It will look quite liquid at this stage but that's fine. The potatoes should be cooked by now. Test them with the point of a knife and when very tender drain them and return the pan to the heat for 1–2 minutes to dry them off. Mash them with the remaining butter, plenty of pepper and about 3 tablespoons of the creamy cooking liquid from the fish. Give the potatoes a good beat and taste for seasoning.

Dollop the mashed potatoes over the fish. It doesn't matter if some of it drops to the bottom rather than sitting on top. Pop the dish under a hot grill for a few minutes until the potato is golden then eat immediately. If you make the fish pie ahead and it has been in the fridge, reheat it in a hot oven for 15–20 minutes or until piping hot.

Salmon Roasted with a Spiced Crumb Crust
Serves 2

A fresh fillet of fish pan-fried or roasted in hot butter with a squeeze of lemon is hard to better. It's one of the simplest of suppers and I'm not one for doing – or suggesting – anything more time consuming unless I feel that the end result is worth it. It is here.

Salmon is still one of our most popular fish and I buy it fairly regularly, but the farmed variety has undoubtedly lost some of its character and needs a bit of help. The marriage of crispy fried breadcrumbs, fresh lime and tender flakes of roasted fish makes this supper well worth the extra effort.

Both the flavoured butter and the fried breadcrumb topping can be made ahead and frozen. They can also be used straight from the freezer so supper can be cooked and ready in under 20 minutes.

2.5cm/1 inch piece fresh root ginger, peeled and grated
large pinch finely chopped red chilli*
75g/3oz unsalted butter, softened
finely grated rind of 1 lime
small palmful roughly chopped coriander, basil or parsley
2 slices good white bread
25g/1oz salted, roasted peanuts
2 spring onions, roughly chopped
salt and freshly ground black pepper
2 salmon fillets, skinned, about 175g/6oz each and 2.5cm/1
    inch thick

Mash the ginger and chilli into the butter with the lime rind and chopped herbs. It's easy to do with a fork and the flavoured butter can be left looking quite rough. Halve the 'bald' lime and set aside.

Put the bread in a processor or blender and whiz into rough breadcrumbs. Add the peanuts and spring onions and whiz again until everything is roughly chopped and blended together. It should look quite chunky. Preheat the oven to 200C/400F/gas mark 6. Melt half of the flavoured butter in a non-stick frying pan and fry the breadcrumb mixture until golden brown. This should only take about 5 minutes or so but stir the crumbs continuously so as not to let them burn. Remove the pan from the heat and season with salt and a generous grinding of black pepper.

Put the salmon fillets, skinned side up in a small, shallow roasting tin and spoon the fried breadcrumbs on top. The fillets should be pretty much covered. Roast for 10–15 minutes or until the salmon is just cooked. To test, slip the point of a knife into the side of one fillet. Push the flakes of fish apart a little. They should be tender and opaque but still very moist.

Meanwhile melt the remaining flavoured butter in the frying pan (no need to wash it) and spoon it around the cooked salmon as you are serving it. Squeeze over the reserved lime and tuck in.

*Fresh chilli is not essential; a pinch of dried chilli powder or a few dried chilli flakes will work just as well but the melted butter will not have the bright speckle of red through it.

Thai Prawn Cakes
Serves 2

With Thai cooking you either love its fragrant, fresh and often fiery flavours or you don't. I love it. The sweet, hot, aromatic taste is quite addictive; so much so that there are times when I just have to have a fix of Thai food. This, I confess, is usually enjoyed in our local Thai restaurant as so many of the dishes involve lengthy lists of ingredients which regular readers of my column will know I try to avoid. However, these little fish cakes are both short and simple. They're also mildly hot and very easy on the palate so even if you think you might not like Thai food, do try them.

I'm not sure that you need the very best prawns for this but I do prefer to buy them ready-cooked in the shell rather than the watery frozen ones. You'll need about 350g/12oz to yield 225g/8oz when shelled. You'll also need 2 stalks of lemon grass, as only the green heart of each stalk is usable. Be ruthless and make sure that you peel away all the outer papery skins leaving just the core to chop.

> 1 shallot, roughly chopped
> ½ large red chilli, de-seeded and chopped
> 2 garlic cloves
> 2 stalks lemon grass, roughly chopped
> 1 tablespoon Thai fish sauce
> small handful coriander leaves
> 225g/8oz cooked, peeled prawns
> 225g/8oz skinned white fish fillet, very roughly chopped
> oil for frying

Put the shallot, chilli, garlic, lemon grass, fish sauce and coriander leaves in the bowl of a food processor and whiz them together for a few seconds until coarsely chopped. Tip the mixture into a bowl.

Next put the prawns and white fish together in the processor (no need to wash out the bowl) and blend them together to a very coarse paste. Add this to the coriander mixture and stir together by hand or with a wooden spoon until just mixed but still quite rough.

With wet hands loosely shape the fish mixture into about 8 rough patties. Drizzle a little oil over the base of a shallow pan (a non-stick pan is the best bet here) and heat until it begins to shimmer. Add the little prawn cakes 2 or 3 at a time and fry in the hot oil until golden and crisp on the outside, about 3–4 minutes on each side. A flat metal slice or palette knife will make life easier when turning the cakes.

Serve them hot with wedges of fresh lime to squeeze on top, some boiled rice and the following Sweet and Sour Coriander Dressing which could also be tossed through some peppery salad leaves.

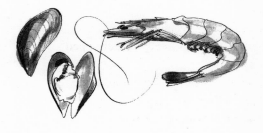

Sweet and Sour Coriander Dressing
Serves 2

6 tablespoons rice wine vinegar
4 tablespoons light soft brown sugar
1 tablespoon soy sauce
red chilli to taste
small handful coriander leaves
juice of 1 lime

Heat the vinegar and sugar together in a small saucepan until the sugar has dissolved. Bring to the boil and bubble for a few minutes until it has turned syrupy. Stir in the soy sauce and leave to cool. Add the chilli, coriander and lime juice.

Crumbed Mackerel with Crispy Bacon
Serves 2

I love the crunch of crispy breadcrumbs on fried fish especially if a little bit of smoky bacon has been added to the pan. Any fishmonger worth his salt will be happy to remove the heads and tails for you and to remove the backbones of the fish so that they're ready to dip in the crumbs.

2 medium-sized mackerel, cleaned and backbone removed
1 small egg, beaten
about 125g/4oz dried white breadcrumbs
4 rashers smoked streaky bacon
oil
knob of butter

Press the fish down along the backbone to flatten out. Dip them into the egg and then the breadcrumbs until well-coated. In a large frying pan cook the bacon rashers until they are very crispy then lift them out of the pan and set aside. Add a drizzle of oil and a small knob of butter to the bacon fat in the pan and add the mackerel. Cook over a fairly high heat for about 2–3 minutes on each side until the breadcrumbs are golden and crispy. Serve the mackerel with the crispy bacon crumbled on top.

Roasted Fish with Warm Potato
and Tarragon Salad
Serves 2

This is a really tasty and trouble-free supper combining roasted fish with a buttery new potato and herb salad. I've been deliberately vague about which variety of fish to use, as it doesn't really matter. Use cod, haddock, hake or hoki – whatever is freshest on the day: they all cook in much the same time. Most fresh herbs will work well too with the exception of the more powerful varieties such as sage or spiky rosemary. I've used tarragon as I love its aromatic aniseed flavour with the fish and the buttery juices of the salad but the fresh taste of flat leaf parsley or dill would be just as good.

    salt and freshly ground black pepper
    125g/4oz small, waxy salad potatoes
    2 thick fillets or steaks of white fish, with skin
    olive oil
    a large knob of butter, about 50g/2oz
    small bunch fresh tarragon
    small glass of dry white wine
    1 hard-boiled egg, shelled and finely chopped

Preheat the oven to 220C/425F/gas mark 7. Bring a pan of water to the boil, add salt then drop in the potatoes. Bubble for about 12–15 minutes or until the potatoes are just tender then drain well.

While the potatoes are cooking, season the fish generously with salt and pepper. Put a drizzle of oil and a little knob of the butter in a small frying pan just large enough to hold the fish in a single layer. (It's going in the oven so make sure that the handle is heatproof or use a small roasting tin.) Heat together until the butter begins to bubble then put the fish, skin side down, into the pan. Cook the fish over a brisk heat for one or two minutes until the skin is golden brown and beginning to crisp then turn it over and tuck a few sprigs of the tarragon under each piece. Dot with a little more butter then pour over the wine. Transfer to the oven and roast for about 8 minutes or until the fish is just tender.

Finely chop the remaining tarragon. Remove the fish from the oven and lift it out of the cooking juices with a slotted spoon. Return to the turned-off oven to keep warm.

Lift the tarragon sprigs out of the cooking juices and discard. Add the potatoes to the pan, place over the hob and bring the liquid to the boil. Bubble for 3–4 minutes until it has reduced to about 3 tablespoons, then off the heat swirl in the remaining butter, chopped tarragon and egg. Taste the buttery mixture – it may need a little more salt and pepper – then spoon around the fish and eat immediately.

A few leaves of peppery watercress could accompany the fish and potato salad, or even some French beans, but you won't need much.

Mussels in Cider and Saffron Broth
Serves 2

A precarious pile of steaming mussels sitting on a creamy, aromatic broth with plenty of crusty bread for dunking is my idea of a feast. This is the dish I love to cook when I've time to linger over supper, for half the joy of it is opening up the shiny blue-black shells to reach the mussels and savouring every mouthful. Getting my fingers messy with the garlicky liquor is all part of the enjoyment too. Large cloth napkins (paper ones will just go soggy) and finger bowls are a must.

My fishmonger sells his mussels in kilo bags, which is, I think, ideal for two people.

1 kilo (about 2lb) mussels (the small blue-black ones please
    not the large green-lipped mussels)
a large knob of butter
2 small shallots, finely chopped
1 small garlic clove, crushed
150ml/5fl oz dry cider
a good pinch saffron threads
ground black pepper
small handful parsley, roughly chopped
about 4 tablespoons double cream or a 150ml/5fl oz carton
    double cream, depending on taste and diet

Tip the mussels into a sink of cold water and take a good look at each one. Throw away any that float, and the rest should be clean and tightly shut with perfect shells, no chips or cracks. If any are open, tap them firmly on the edge of the sink and they should close slowly. Throw away any that don't. Under a running tap, pull the coarse beard off each mussel by giving it a good firm tug, then cover them with fresh cold water while you prepare the broth.

Melt the butter in a large saucepan and cook the shallot with the garlic until they are soft and golden. Don't rush this – uncooked shallot will spoil the finished broth. Add the cider, saffron strands and a good grinding of black pepper.

Allow the liquid to come to the boil then throw in all but a tablespoon of the parsley and all the mussels. Cover the pan with a lid or baking sheet and let the mussels steam for about 2–3 minutes or until all the shells have opened. Throw away any shells that are still tightly shut. Once the heat has opened the majority of the shells the mussels are cooked. Don't be tempted to give them a few minutes longer or you'll be left with inedible rubber.

Scoop the mussels out with a slotted spoon and tip into warmed serving bowls. Quickly return the pan to the heat and stir in as much cream as you want to. Bring the liquor to the boil; bubble furiously for 1–2 minutes then pour it over the mussels. Throw in the remaining parsley and rush to the table. Eat while steaming hot.

Note: mussels are available all year now thanks to foreign imports but they do have an 'off season' over the summer months when they're spawning. At home this is usually anywhere from around March/April to July/August.

Grilled Salmon with Lemon and Caper Butter Sauce

Serves 2

'Sauces for fish, please.' This is one of the most regular requests I receive in my postbag but I confess that I rarely do anything too fancy with fish. However, here is one favourite sauce that I believe is worth the little bit of extra effort and it doesn't take a great deal of time. You may not need all the sauce that this recipe makes but it's impossible to produce less in a blender. If you do have any left over it will keep in the fridge for about 4–5 days. Stir the cold sauce into hot green beans or boiled potatoes and serve them just as the butter begins to melt.

2 large egg yolks
125g/4oz butter
2 teaspoons white wine vinegar
juice of 1 lemon, about 2–3 tablespoons
about 2 tablespoons capers, chopped
2 salmon fillets, about 175g/6oz each
salt and freshly ground black pepper

Whiz the egg yolks in a blender or food processor for about 10 seconds then melt the butter in a small saucepan over a low heat. Put the vinegar and half the lemon juice in a separate pan and bring to the boil. With the blender motor running, add the hot vinegar mixture to the egg yolks. Increase the heat under the butter and when it starts to bubble add it immediately to the egg yolk mixture in a thin, steady stream. Keep the blender whizzing and when all the hot butter has been added the sauce should be the thickness of lightly whipped cream (the heat of the butter cooks the egg yolks a little and thickens them). Spoon the sauce into a small bowl and stir in the capers. Taste the sauce now; you may need to add a little salt and a bit more lemon juice to your taste. I like the sauce quite sharp, especially with salmon.

Now, place the salmon fillets skin side up on a baking sheet. Season with salt and plenty of pepper, then squeeze over the remaining lemon juice. Cook the salmon under a preheated grill for 3–4 minutes depending on the thickness of the fillets. Get the fish quite close to the heat so that the skin chars a little in places. There is no need to turn the fish over – it will cook through and remain juicy inside. Push a skewer or the point of a knife into the fillet to see if it is cooked. The fish should break into flakes easily. Serve the hot salmon with a spoonful of the warm butter sauce on top.

Note: If you don't like capers the butter sauce is just as good if you flavour it with tarragon, chives or dill. You'll need about 2 teaspoons of the chopped herb. Try the sauce with steamed asparagus or a pan-fried steak too.

Salt-baked Trout
Serves 2

Another good, easy recipe that needs next to no preparation.
The fish is covered in a thick salt coat then baked so that it
emerges from the oven moist and full of flavour. I think trout
works especially well but try it with mackerel too. Buy the trout
from a fishmonger or from the wet fish counter in the supermarket, and if you want the heads and tails removed ask them
to do it for you.

about 350g/12oz sea salt
2 garlic cloves, crushed
2 trout, cleaned

Preheat the oven to 220C/425F/gas mark 7. Line a roasting tin
with foil and add enough of the salt to make a 1.25cm/½ inch
thick layer. Sprinkle over the garlic. Push the trout down into
the tin then cover completely with the remaining salt. Press it
down well. Bake the fish for about 20 minutes. Remove from
the oven and crack the salt to open.

Serve whilst hot with Crème Fraîche and Horseradish Sauce
and chunks of lemon.

Crème Fraîche and Horseradish Sauce

This is the simplest of sauces and one that is pretty good with grilled mackerel and plain roast beef too.

200ml tub crème fraîche
1 teaspoon hot creamed horseradish
1 garlic clove, crushed
salt and freshly ground black pepper

Put all the ingredients in a small saucepan and slowly bring to the boil. Reduce the heat to a gentle bubble and leave the sauce to reduce a little for about 3–4 minutes. Serve warm.

Scallops with Sweet Chilli Sauce
Serves 2

I always believed the best way to enjoy scallops was to pan fry them in sizzling butter, oil and garlic then serve them with chunks of lemon: the ultimate ten-minute supper. Anything more elaborate and painstaking I considered just not worth the effort. That is until I ate Peter Gordon's Scallops with Sweet Chilli Sauce. I shall be eternally grateful to Peter, chef of London's The Sugar Club restaurant, for creating this recipe. The citrus flavour of the lemon grass, sweetness of the caramel and fragrance of the coriander make the sauce quite addictive.

It's fiddlier than my usual suppers, it requires far more ingredients than I would normally want to use and it's also more expensive than most midweek meals. But – if you're planning a treat for St Valentine's night or a special occasion, it's a memorable supper for two. This is my slightly adapted version of Peter's dish.

sesame oil
6–8 large scallops, depending on appetite
salt and freshly ground black pepper
crème fraîche

For the sweet chilli sauce
4 plump garlic cloves, peeled
1 large red chilli, de-seeded and roughly chopped
1 thumb-sized piece fresh root ginger, peeled and roughly
    chopped
4 kaffir lime leaves (if you can't find these the sauce is still
    good without)
1 large handful fresh coriander leaves
2 stalks lemon grass
100ml/4fl oz cider or white wine vinegar

50ml/2fl oz Thai fish sauce
50ml/2fl oz soy sauce
125g/4oz caster sugar

To make the sauce put the garlic, chilli, ginger, lime leaves and coriander in the bowl of a food processor. Remove the outer first and possibly second leaf from the lemon grass and trim off the top third of the stems. This leaves the freshest, greenest part of the stalk. Roughly chop it and add to the other ingredients. Whiz everything together to a coarse paste. Measure the vinegar, fish sauce and soy sauce into a jug.

Put the sugar in a heavy-based saucepan with 4 tablespoons of water. Leave the pan over a very gentle heat until all the sugar has dissolved. This may take 10–12 minutes but don't let the mixture bubble until the sugar has dissolved. When it has, increase the heat and bubble the sugar furiously for about 5–7 minutes until it turns a dark golden caramel. Stir in the paste and the measured liquid. Lean away from the pan as you do this as the caramel splutters and throws up a pungent steam. Bring the mixture back to the boil and stir until the caramel has dissolved and the sauce has reduced to a sticky syrup. Set aside (the sauce can be made to this stage a day ahead and kept in a cool place).

Lightly oil the scallops with sesame oil and season with salt and plenty of pepper. Heat a frying pan or griddle until scorching hot then drop in the scallops. They should sizzle immediately if the pan is hot enough. Leave them alone for about 1 minute or until you can see that they have formed a golden crust on the underside. Turn the scallops over and cook for a further minute. They should still be springy if you press one with your finger.

Serve the scallops immediately with stir-fried Chinese greens, the warm sweet chilli sauce and a small bowl of chilled crème fraîche to dollop on top. Bliss!

Salmon in a Puff of Pastry
Serves 2

I'm not the patient cook I used to be. Homemade puff pastry and elaborately latticed salmon suppers are no longer on my agenda. I still love the combination of creamy salmon inside crisp and flaky pastry but I just don't feel inclined to fiddle any more. This supper is just as good to eat as any carefully crimped salmon-en-croûte, yet armed with a sheet of ready-rolled puff pastry it can be made and in the oven in minutes. Nothing can ever better the flavour of a home-made pastry but all the supermarket ones are pretty good especially if you roll them out a little thinner so that they're crisp and golden when cooked.

1 shallot, finely chopped
a knob of butter
1 sheet of ready-rolled puff pastry
4 tablespoons mascarpone cheese
1 teaspoon Dijon mustard
1 tablespoon chopped fresh dill, tarragon, chives or parsley
salt and ground black pepper
2 thick salmon fillets, cut from the centre of the fish
1 beaten egg
lemon wedges

Put the shallot into a small pan with the butter. Cook it slowly over a moderate heat for about 5–7 minutes or until it is soft and pale golden. Spoon the shallot and the butter into a small bowl and leave to cool. Preheat the oven to 200C/400F/gas mark 6. Allow the puff pastry to come to room temperature then unroll and lay it out flat on a lightly floured work surface. Roll the pastry sheet out a little thinner until you have a rough 30.5cm/12 inch square. Cut the pastry in half lengthways then into quarters. Put a baking sheet into the hot oven to heat up.

Beat the cold shallot and butter mixture into the mascarpone with the mustard, herbs and plenty of seasoning.

Put a salmon fillet in the centre of two of the pastry squares with a heaped spoonful of the mascarpone mixture on top. Dampen the pastry edges with the beaten egg brushing the egg right up to the edge of the salmon. Lay the remaining two squares on top and press down firmly to seal in the filling. Trim the pastry into a neat square close to the salmon edges. Brush all over with the remaining beaten egg then, using a fish slice, transfer the pastries to the hot baking sheet.

Cook for about 20 minutes or until the pastry is puffed and golden then serve immediately with lemon wedges to squeeze over the salmon when the pastry is cut open. This last minute squeeze of lemon juice gives an extra edge to the sauce.

Try serving some spinach with this salmon. The wilted leaves are delicious when they've mingled with the buttery herb sauce.

Wash four good handfuls of spinach leaves, even if they come from a neatly packed supermarket bag. The leaves need a little water clinging to them to steam rather than fry. Put the spinach in a large saucepan with plenty of salt, pepper and a grating of nutmeg. Stir the leaves gently over a moderate heat until they just begin to soften and wilt then serve them straight away.

Baked Plaice with Polenta Crumbs
Serves 2

2 tablespoons polenta
knob of butter, melted
2 large plaice fillets, skin on
2 teaspoons finely grated Parmesan cheese
salt and ground black pepper
Fresh Tomato & Chilli Sauce

Put the polenta in a small bowl and add about 4 tablespoons cold water. Set this aside to soak for 2–3 minutes until the water has been absorbed. Brush half the melted butter over the base of a heatproof dish just large enough to hold the plaice in a single layer and put the fish on top skin-side up.

Mix the soaked polenta with the Parmesan cheese and add a little salt and plenty of pepper. Now pop the fish under a hot grill for 3 minutes or until the skin begins to bubble and turn golden. Carefully turn the fish over and brush it with the remaining melted butter. Spread with the polenta mixture (if the polenta has become too stiff add a little extra water to soften) and return to the grill for a further 3–4 minutes or until the topping is crisp and golden. Serve with Fresh Tomato and Chilli Sauce.

Fresh Tomato and Chilli Sauce
Serves 2

It's vital to use soft ripe tomatoes in this recipe to ensure it's big on flavour and that there is enough natural juice for the finished sauce.

225g/8oz very ripe tomatoes, preferably on the vine, roughly chopped
3 shallots, finely chopped
2 garlic cloves, crushed
½ red chilli, split and seeds removed
salt and ground black pepper
1 teaspoon caster sugar or clear honey
palmful chopped fresh basil

Place the first four ingredients in a small saucepan and bring to the boil. Reduce the heat to a slow simmer and cook for about 15–20 minutes or until it is the consistency of soft chutney.

Remove the chilli then season to taste with salt, pepper and sugar. Stir the basil into the sauce and serve.

Coconut Fish Curry
Serves 2

This is a very straightforward curry recipe that's ready to serve in around 30 minutes. There are plenty of creamy coconut juices so serve the dish with rice or naan bread to soak them up.

a large knob of fresh root ginger, peeled and roughly
    chopped
3 garlic cloves, crushed
corn or grapeseed oil
1 small onion, sliced
about 2 teaspoons ground cumin
a large pinch ground turmeric
a pinch of dried chilli flakes
200ml/7fl oz coconut milk
salt and freshly ground black pepper
2 chunky fillets of fish, about 175g/6oz each

Put the ginger and garlic in a blender with 150ml/5fl oz water and whiz until quite smooth. Heat a drizzle of oil in a large frying pan and add the onion. Cook for a good 7–10 minutes or until the onion is soft and beginning to turn golden. Stir in the cumin, turmeric and chilli, and cook over the heat for about 30 seconds. Add the ginger liquid from the blender with the coconut milk and seasoning. Bring to the boil and bubble until the liquid reduces by about half. Cut the fish into large bite-size pieces (any smaller and it will disintegrate in the pan) and drop into the hot sauce. Simmer very gently for 4–5 minutes or until the fish is very lightly cooked. Serve immediately.

CHAPTER 2

Chicken and Game

Lemon and Sesame Chicken
Serves 2

Please don't be put off by the long list of ingredients. It should only take about 10 minutes to prepare and even less time to cook!

2 chicken breast fillets, cut into bite-size strips
1 stalk lemon grass, finely chopped
finely grated rind and juice of 1 lime
2 fat garlic cloves, crushed
125g/4oz shallots, thinly sliced
1 tablespoon Thai fish sauce
1 teaspoon light soft brown sugar
½ small red chilli, de-seeded and finely chopped
1 tablespoon sesame oil
2 teaspoons sesame seeds
light oil, such as grapeseed oil
lime wedges and Chinese pancakes, noodles or steamed rice
    to serve

Mix together all the ingredients in a large non-metallic bowl. If you have the time, cover the bowl and leave the chicken to marinate in the fridge for 2–3 hours.

Wipe the surface of a large wok with a little oil and place over a high heat until smoky hot. Stir-fry the chicken mixture, just a few pieces at a time, for 3–4 minutes or until the pieces are golden brown and cooked through. If you try to cook too many pieces at once the chicken will stew rather than fry. Return all the chicken to the wok and toss it together over the heat for a further minute. Serve immediately with lime wedges to squeeze over and wrap in warm Chinese pancakes or toss into egg noodles or accompany with plain steamed rice.

Mustard and Basil Chicken
Serves 2

Chicken is one of those ingredients where you get what you pay for. A good free-range chicken may be pricey but it will reward you with a richer, meatier flavour than any intensively reared bird.

The magic of this chicken supper is that it needs very few ingredients and is endlessly variable.

Most of the large supermarkets now have fresh herbs all year round but if you are unable to find fresh basil blend 2 tablespoons of chopped fresh parsley and about 4 teaspoons good quality pesto sauce with the mustard and vinegar. If all you have in the storecupboard is the vinegar and mustard, blend those with half the oil and it's still very good! If you have time to make the sauce the night before you could spoon a little of it over the chicken, then cover it with clingfilm and leave to marinate in the fridge overnight.

2 free-range chicken breasts on the bone and with skin
a large handful of fresh basil
6 anchovy fillets, about half a can
4 tablespoons red wine vinegar
4 teaspoons Dijon mustard
175ml/6fl oz olive oil

Ease up the skin from each piece of chicken and push 1 or 2 basil leaves underneath (this isn't absolutely essential but does add to the flavour of the chicken). Put the remaining basil leaves in a food processor with the anchovy fillets, vinegar and mustard and whiz together for about 10 seconds to make a rough paste. With the motor running, slowly pour in the olive oil. Reserve about half of this mustard sauce and put the remainder in a small serving bowl.

Heat the grill to its highest setting; lay the chicken skin side down in the grill pan and spoon over about half of the reserved mustard sauce. Cook the chicken about 5cm/2 inches away from the heat for about 7 minutes. Turn the chicken over skin side up and spoon over the remaining mustard sauce. Baste with the cooking juices, which will look a little curdled now but don't worry! Cook for a further 6–7 minutes until the chicken is crisp, lightly charred and cooked through.

Serve the chicken with the grill pan juices and the remaining cold mustard and vinegar sauce.

Sticky Chicken
Serves 2

Imagine my delight when I heard that spices, about which I'm something of a fanatic, are positively good for me. This is no surprise to most Indians of course who have long believed that the simple combination of turmeric, ginger and garlic is a particularly beneficial one for its antiseptic qualities.

I love to use chicken thighs for this recipe; they have a good meaty flavour and stay moist and juicy under the grill. Most supermarkets sell ready-boned thighs but invariably without the skin which I find infuriating. Chicken grilled or roasted without the skin is unthinkable. So for this recipe I buy whole thighs and bone them myself (it's not as fiddly as it sounds), or I buy them from my butcher and he bones them for me. If you can't find fresh mint don't worry, the chicken is just as good without.

    1 teaspoon ground turmeric
    1 tablespoon light oil, such as groundnut
    2 tablespoons runny honey
    6 boned, free-range chicken thighs, with skin
    1 small onion, thinly sliced from root to tip
    2 fat garlic cloves, thinly sliced
    small knob of fresh root ginger, about the size of a walnut,
        peeled and shredded
    about a dozen fresh mint leaves, roughly torn

In a glass or metal bowl make a thin paste with the turmeric, oil and honey. Cut the chicken into strips, roughly the size of a thick finger, and stir them into the spice paste. Add the onion, garlic, ginger and most of the mint. Toss with the chicken and leave as long as you can, at least twenty minutes, for the chicken to soak up some of the flavours.

Remove the wire rack from the grill pan and line the pan with foil. Tip the chicken mixture into the pan and spread out into an even layer. Preheat the grill and when it is as hot as possible put the chicken about 5cm/2 inches away from the heat. Cook for about 10 minutes turning and basting the mixture every 2–3 minutes as the honey caramelizes. Lift the grill pan closer to the heat for the last 2–3 minutes of cooking to help crisp the chicken skin. The chicken is ready when it's golden brown, a little blackened and firm to the touch.

Scatter over the remaining mint, sprinkle with a little salt and serve with chunks of lemon.

The chicken is particularly good stuffed into warm pitta bread, kebab-style, or spooned onto a bed of well-buttered couscous speckled with sultanas and toasted almonds or pinenuts.

Roast Chicken with Garlic and Wine
Serves 2

Can a recipe ever be too simple? I don't think so. I buy chicken every week as most of us do and this is one of my regular suppers with a few variations according to what else is in the fridge. As with all simple recipes, the quality of the ingredients is vital. I buy free-range chicken breasts from my local butcher which are more expensive than the ordinary supermarket ones but they have bags of flavour, need very little added and are worth every penny. A good piece of chicken roasted quite simply with olive oil, butter and garlic produces the most gorgeous savoury juices. With a splash of white wine and a little extra butter whisked in you can create a delicious mellow sauce flavoured with the caramelized sweetness of roasted garlic. But do annoy your butcher, as I do, by insisting on chicken with skin. It keeps the chicken moist as it cooks and is wonderfully crisp and salty to eat. Chicken without it just isn't worth cooking – or eating.

> 2 free-range chicken breast fillets on the bone and with skin
> large knob salted butter
> salt and ground black pepper
> 2 garlic cloves, peeled and sliced
> olive oil
> a wine glass of white wine

Preheat the oven to 200C/400F/gas mark 6. Put the chicken breasts skin-side up in a small roasting tin just large enough to hold the chicken comfortably. Too large a tin and the pan juices, which are vital for the finished sauce, will just evaporate away; too small and the chicken will stew rather than roast.

Dot each chicken breast with a good knob of butter and season well with salt and plenty of pepper. Scatter over the sliced garlic then drizzle everything with a little olive oil and roast for about 25 minutes depending on the size of the chicken pieces. Free-range portions do tend to be larger so may take an extra 5–10 minutes. Baste with the pan juices about half way through the cooking time.

Remove the chicken from the roasting tin and keep warm (at this stage, if you feel that the skin isn't crispy enough pop the chicken under a hot grill for 2–3 minutes while you finish the sauce).

The roasting tin should have at least 4–5 tablespoons of cooking juices in it. Put it over a fairly high heat on the hob and whisk in about a wine glass of white wine. It will come to the boil quickly and as it does, scrape up the sticky bits from the bottom of the pan and whisk them into the juices. With the liquid still bubbling take a knob of butter on the end of the whisk and add it to the pan. Keep whisking until the butter has melted completely. Taste the sauce and stop here or add a bit more butter if you're feeling extravagant. It shouldn't need any more seasoning. Serve the chicken with the buttery juices spooned on top.

Try . . .

• Tucking 2 or 3 crushed fresh tarragon leaves under the chicken skin before adding the salt, pepper and butter.

• Sprinkling a little freshly grated Parmesan cheese over the cooked chicken and grill for 2–3 minutes while finishing the sauce.

• Adding a few finely chopped brown cap mushrooms to the cooking juices before adding the wine and finish with a tablespoon of cream or crème fraîche.

• Using a pure, unsweetened apple juice if you don't want to use wine.

Grilled Lemon and Ginger Chicken
Serves 2

Chicken is always on my weekly shopping list but most of the time I buy it because I know it's going to make a quick supper not because I've any idea in mind about how I'm going to cook it. I'd like to say that this recipe has become a regular because it produces moist, golden chicken with a zingy little sauce but if I'm honest it's more probably because it needs only a couple of fresh ingredients that I usually have to hand. It also has the added advantage of being equally great hot or cold — a definite bonus during one of our unpredictable summers.

2 small thin-skinned lemons
1 stalk lemon grass
1 piece fresh root ginger, peeled and thinly sliced
2 generous tablespoons caster sugar
2 free-range chicken breast fillets (with skin)
salt and ground black pepper

Halve the lemons and squeeze the juice into a small saucepan (don't throw away the lemon shells as they're going to be used later). Split open the lemon grass stalk from tip to root. Only the green heart of the stalk is usable so be ruthless and make sure that you peel away all the outer papery skins leaving just the core then chop it quite finely. Add to the pan with the ginger and sugar then pour in 300ml/½ pint water and give it all a good stir. Put the pan over a low heat and stir for 4–5 minutes until all the sugar has dissolved then increase the heat and bring it to the boil. Bubble the liquid until it has reduced down by about half and is quite syrupy; it should take just 10 minutes. (This syrup can be made a day or so ahead and kept in the fridge.)

Season the chicken with salt and a generous grinding of

black pepper and place skin side down in a small, shallow roasting tin that's just large enough to hold the chicken pieces comfortably. Strain over the sugar syrup and add the squeezed lemon halves.

Get the grill really hot and place the chicken about 15–20cm/6–8 inches away from the heat. Cook for about 7–8 minutes, basting with the syrup. Turn the chicken over, baste again with the syrup, and raise the pan to about 10cm/4 inches away from the heat. Cook for a further 4–5 minutes or until the chicken is tender all the way through, the skin crisp and the syrup a golden sticky sauce.

Eat with boiled rice flecked with chopped coriander or with a rice salad. Mango with Lime and Chilli (see page 40) makes a good accompaniment with the chicken whether it's served hot or cold.

Mango with Lime and Chilli
Serves 2

Peel and slice or cube a large ripe mango. Add a pinch of finely chopped red chilli and the juice of 1 small lime. If the mango isn't fully ripe add a tiny pinch of soft brown sugar. Toss together and serve with the grilled chicken.

Chicken, Bean and Spinach Curry
Serves 2

The supermarket shelves are brimming over with ready-made sauces, some good and some not so good. I never feel guilty about using some of the better ones – with a few added extras they can form the base of a great supper.

If you have any leftover cream in the fridge add 1 or 2 spoonfuls with the yoghurt for an extra creamy sauce.

light oil, such as grapeseed
175g/6oz chicken or turkey fillet strips
1 garlic clove
125g ready-made curry sauce, such as Loyd Grossman's
    Korma
75g/3oz cooked green lentils or aduki beans, drained and
    rinsed
small carton natural bio yoghurt
50g/2oz ready prepared spinach
handful of coriander leaves

Heat a drizzle of oil in a wok or deep frying pan and fry the chicken strips with the crushed garlic until a good golden brown.

Add the sauce and the lentils then cover and simmer very gently for about 15 minutes or until the chicken is tender.

Over a low heat stir in the yoghurt keeping the curry hot without boiling then stir in the spinach and coriander leaves over the heat until they just begin to wilt. Serve straight away.

Roast Pheasant with Orange and Juniper
Serves 2

I'm very conservative about pheasant. I love it plainly roasted
with butter and served with plenty of good, creamy bread sauce.
For me, meddling with a classic dish such as this rarely pays off.
However, Maggie Beer, one of Australia's most talented chefs,
managed to persuade me otherwise with her pheasant roasted
with orange and juniper. It's a delicious moist and fragrant roast,
and just the sort of thing for a Saturday supper especially with
mashed parsnips – made with a little cream and a good grinding
of pepper.

   a large, plump young pheasant
   finely grated rind and juice of 2 large oranges
   6 juniper berries
   few sprigs fresh thyme
   a large knob of butter
   salt and ground black pepper
   2 capfuls of gin, about 50ml/2fl oz

Put the pheasant in a shallow, non-metallic dish. Stir the orange
rind into the juice then crush the juniper berries between your
fingers and add them to the orange with the thyme sprigs. Pour
the resulting slush over the pheasant and turn the bird in it
several times. Cover the dish and set it aside for a good hour or
two, or leave it overnight if you have the time.

Preheat the oven to 190C/375F/gas mark 5. Lift the
pheasant out of the dish and scrape any marinade still clinging
to it back into the dish. Melt the butter in a shallow roasting tin
or casserole just large enough to hold the pheasant with just a
little 'breathing' space around it (too small and the bird will stew
rather than roast but too large a tin will allow the pan juices to
evaporate away).

When the butter starts to sizzle lightly fry the pheasant breast side down, until the skin is golden brown all over. Do this slowly so that the butter does not burn, a matter of 3–4 minutes.

Take the pan off the heat and season the bird with a few grinds of salt and pepper. Pour the marinade mixture back over the pheasant and add the gin. Keep the bird breast side down and roast in the hot oven for 30 minutes. Turn the pheasant breast side up and baste with the pan juices, which should be a deep caramel colour by now. Pour the juices off into a small saucepan and keep warm then return the pheasant to the oven for a further 15–20 minutes depending on the size of bird (pierce a thigh with a skewer and the juices should run clear). Remove from the oven and leave to rest for about 10 minutes before serving.

Carve the pheasant if you wish though I prefer to cut it in half along the backbone and down the breastbone (you'll need a good strong knife or a pair of stout scissors for this). Taste the pan juices and add any extra seasoning needed, then pour in any liquid from the resting bird. Make sure the juices are hot then spoon over the roast pheasant and serve immediately with mashed parsnips.

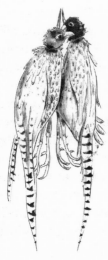

Tray-baked Chicken and Artichoke Supper
Serves 2

What has happened to the Jerusalem artichoke? The knobbly
tubers I remember cursing as I peeled years ago were as lumpy
as the roughest root ginger; now there's hardly a bump to be
seen. But in spite of this transformation it is still one of the most
underrated vegetables on the greengrocer's shelf. I suspect this
is largely due to its continuing high flatulence factor but I love
this winter gem with its earthy flavour. It's well worth trying and
suffering the after-effects.

    a large knob of butter
    2 large chicken breasts (with skin still on)
    1 large onion, finely sliced
    about 350g/12oz Jerusalem artichokes
    1 fat garlic clove
    small palmful of chopped fresh thyme
    175ml/6fl oz chicken stock and dry white wine mixed, about
        half and half
    plenty of salt and ground black pepper
    3 large tablespoons double cream

Preheat the oven to 190C/375F/gas mark 5. Warm the butter
in a small roasting tin until it melts then add the chicken, skin-
side down, and leave it undisturbed over a high heat for two to
three minutes or until the skin is golden brown. Take care not
to let the butter burn. If it looks as though it might then add a
drizzle of olive oil to the pan. Remove the chicken and set aside.
Turn the heat down then throw in the onion. Cook it, stirring
from time to time, until it is soft and translucent. While it is
cooking, which will take a good 10–15 minutes, peel the
artichokes. This is easiest to do with a swivel parer and best left
to the last minute or they will very quickly turn a sad shade of

brown. Slice them into rounds about the thickness of a pound coin.

When the onions are soft and just beginning to turn golden, stir in the crushed garlic, thyme and artichokes. Continue to cook, stirring over the heat, until the artichokes are coated in buttery onions and they are beginning to turn golden. Next pour in the stock and wine mixture, scraping up any crusty bits from the bottom of the tin. Leave the tin over the heat until the liquid comes to the boil then leave to bubble gently for about five minutes, adding salt and plenty of black pepper. Take the tin off the heat and stir in the cream.

Put the browned chicken breasts, skin-side up, on the artichoke mixture pushing them down a little into the liquid then bake everything together in the hot oven for about 45 minutes or until tender, golden and bubbling. The cooking time will depend on the thickness of the artichokes. If the chicken breasts are small add them to the artichokes after 15 minutes cooking time.

Try . . .

• Frying the sliced or chopped artichokes in the butter with the garlic and thyme until tender and golden then add salt, plenty of pepper and squeeze over half a small lemon before serving.

Slow-simmered Chicken
with Apple and Lentils
Serves 2

There's something incredibly comforting about food that is slowly cooked in the oven. It's also incredibly easy. This recipe is often my choice for lunch on a busy Sunday when I'm not sure when we're going to sit down and eat. An extra half-hour in the oven won't matter. Please don't think that the parsley added at the end of cooking time is just for garnish – it's not. Parsley is such an abused herb, it breaks my heart to see it thrown willy-nilly onto a plate. Its clean, earthy flavour can perk up many otherwise dull dishes.

1 tablespoon oil
2 chicken breast quarters or 4 thighs
225g/8oz baby carrots, pared and trimmed
125g/4oz baby parsnips, pared and trimmed
125g/4oz thin leeks, washed and thickly sliced
175g/6oz button onions, peeled and trimmed
pinch chopped fresh sage
50g/2oz Puy lentils
1 small Granny Smith apple, cored and thickly sliced
150ml/5fl oz pure unsweetened apple juice
150ml/5fl oz good chicken stock
salt and ground black pepper
handful chopped fresh flatleaf parsley

Preheat the oven to 190C/375F/gas mark 5. Heat the oil in a large flameproof casserole and brown the chicken well, a few pieces at a time. This doesn't mean just a tinge of colour but a good deep golden brown. This is so important for both flavour and colour. Remove from the pan and drain on kitchen paper. Add all the vegetables to the pan and fry them for a good 4–5 minutes. Again, these need to be well coloured. Add the sage (not too much), lentils, apples, apple juice and chicken stock and bring the liquid to the boil. Season generously and return all the chicken. Cover the pot securely with a lid or foil then simmer everything together in the oven for about 1 hour or until the chicken is very tender. Taste for seasoning and stir in the parsley just before serving.

Spiced Saffron Chicken and Figs

Serves 2

Chicken cooked in this way and served with couscous is called a 'tagine' and traditionally requires eight or nine different spices. Our 'midweek' version uses just five but is still packed with flavour. Although it takes an hour to cook it's ready for the oven in just 15 minutes and can be made ahead and re-heated.

2 chicken breast fillets on the bone and with skin
30ml/2 tablespoons oil
2 small onions, peeled and quartered
2.5cm/1 inch piece fresh root ginger, peeled and finely
    chopped
pinch cumin or coriander seeds
large pinch saffron strands
pinch ground turmeric
1 cinnamon stick
125g/4oz ready-to-eat dried figs
salt and freshly ground black pepper
Minted Couscous to accompany

Preheat the oven to 190C/375F/gas mark 5. Use a flameproof casserole just large enough to hold the chicken side by side. Heat the oil in the casserole and fry the onions for a good 10 minutes or until golden and beginning to soften. Add the ginger and fry for 1–2 minutes. Stir in all the spices and fry together for a further 1–2 minutes.

Add the chicken to the casserole fleshy side down, scatter the figs around and pour in 300ml/½ pint boiling water. Season with plenty of salt and pepper then cover tightly and cook in the oven for about 40 minutes. The flesh of the chicken should be moist and falling off the bone. Lift the chicken from the cooking liquid with a slotted spoon. Cover and keep warm in a low oven. The cooking liquid can now be used to make a savoury, herby couscous to serve with the chicken, see page 50.

Minted Couscous

Serves 2

reserved liquid from chicken, see previous recipe
125g/4oz couscous
2.5ml/1 level teaspoon harissa or pinch dried chilli flakes
25g/1oz toasted blanched almonds
small handful golden raisins
small handful chopped fresh parsley
small handful chopped fresh mint
lemon wedges

Return the cooking liquid from the chicken to the boil. Take the pan off the heat and stir in all the ingredients above, except the herbs. Cover with foil and leave to soak for about 10 minutes, by which time the couscous will have absorbed most of the liquid. Stir the herbs in with a fork to fluff up the grains and serve with lemon wedges to squeeze over the couscous.

Roast Chicken with Honey Dressing
Serves 2

Most supermarkets and good butchers sell ready-roasted chickens that are simply irresistible and make summer salads such as this so effortless.

half a warm, ready-roasted chicken
50g/2oz roasted, salted cashew nuts, roughly chopped
75ml/3fl oz vinaigrette
1 teaspoon clear honey
2.5cm/1 inch piece fresh root ginger, finely grated
1 garlic clove, crushed
2.5ml/½ teaspoon ground turmeric
pinch garam masala
salt and freshly ground black pepper
handful of flat leaf parsley, roughly chopped

Divide the chicken into large bite-sized pieces. There's no need to be too neat about this; the warm chicken will tear quite naturally into pieces. Put the chicken on a serving platter and sprinkle over the nuts. Whisk together the vinaigrette with all the remaining ingredients and pour over the warm chicken. Serve immediately.

Crispy Duck with Hot Sweet Dip
Serves 2

If you know you're going to be pushed for time to cook supper one night, this is the perfect answer. Simmer the duck legs and put them in the marinade the night before and they can then be grilled and ready to eat in less than 15 minutes.

  2 small duck legs
  1 piece star anise
  2 fat garlic cloves, peeled and sliced
  ½ red chilli, de-seeded and finely chopped
  grated rind and juice of 1 orange
  2 teaspoons fresh tamarind paste or lemon juice

Prick the duck legs all over with a skewer or fork then put them in a large saucepan with the star anise. Cover with cold water, bring to the boil, then reduce the heat to a gentle bubble and simmer the duck for 45 minutes. Meanwhile mix together all the remaining ingredients.

Drain the duck and discard the star anise. Place the legs, skin side down, on a foil-lined grill pan. Spoon over half the garlic mixture and grill for 5 minutes. Turn the duck skin side up and spoon over the remaining mixture. Grill for a further 5–7 minutes or until the duck skin is well charred and the skin deliciously crispy. Serve the duck on a bed of soft salad leaves to mingle with the hot juices, and with a Hot Sweet Dip.

Hot Sweet Dip
Serves 2

150ml/5fl oz white wine vinegar
45ml/3 tablespoons caster sugar
75g/3oz each, cucumber, spring onion and mango, finely
    chopped or cut into fine shreds
small pinch de-seeded and shredded red chilli or more if you
    wish!

Boil the vinegar and sugar together for 2 minutes, then stir in
all the remaining ingredients. Set aside and leave to cool.

Coconut and Coriander Chicken
Serves 2

A straightforward curry rich with coconut and scented with coriander. It's such a quick and easy dish and a great choice too if having friends to supper. Just double up the quantities. The flavour of coriander is much subtler if it's not chopped too finely, so leave the leaves in large pieces. Finally, if you've never tried sweet potatoes now's the time! They are a cross between a potato and a carrot in both flavour and texture. Try them baked, they take half the time of ordinary potatoes. If you can't find them use old potatoes or carrots or a mixture of both instead.

1 onion, finely chopped
2 tablespoons light oil
2 tablespoons mild curry paste
1 small sweet potato, peeled and chopped into large chunks
200ml/7fl oz coconut milk
1 small can chopped tomatoes
2 skinless chicken breast fillets
salt and freshly ground black pepper
1 small bunch of fresh coriander, roughly chopped

Use a deep frying pan or a shallow, heatproof casserole, as there's quite a bit of sauce. Fry the onion in the oil until soft and golden. Take a good 10 minutes to do this – getting the onion soft and golden brings out its natural 'sweetness' and adds to the flavour of the finished dish. Add the curry paste and sweet potato and stir around in the hot oil for 3–4 minutes. Add the coconut milk, tomatoes and chicken, then cover and simmer very gently for about 20 minutes or until the chicken is tender. Turn the chicken over half way through cooking if the pieces are not completely covered in the sauce. Taste for seasoning then throw in the coriander just before serving.

Try . . . naan bread warm from the grill or the oven to mop up the sauce, and some slices of mango tossed in lime juice. Poppadums are good too. Remember that the ones that need to be cooked can be done in the microwave, which saves the hassle and smell of deep-frying them. Do one at a time and allow about 20–25 seconds on full power.

Full marks . . . to supermarkets that are now selling fresh coriander in large bunches. If you are a fan of the herb like me then 2 or 3 sprigs are never enough.

Oven-baked Chicken with Rosemary and Cracked Garlic

Serves 2

Recipes don't come much quicker than this. When nothing else comes to mind for supper, this is always a marvellous standby.

    2 onions, peeled and cut into large chunks
    1 large baking potato, peeled and cut into large chunks
    about 450g/1lb chicken joints, thighs or breast, skin on
    6–8 garlic cloves, unpeeled
    small handful of rosemary sprigs
    50ml/2fl oz olive oil
    salt and freshly ground black pepper

Put all the ingredients in a medium roasting tin and season well with plenty of salt and pepper. Roast at 220C/425F/gas mark 7 for about 45 minutes or until the chicken and potatoes are golden brown and the onions are caramelized. Turn the chicken and vegetables around once or twice as they cook to get a good even colour.

Roast Chicken with a Devilled Sauce
Serves 2

Although chicken is delicious enough plainly roasted or grilled, the sweet and savoury baste here adds a hot, tangy note.

about 450g/1lb chicken joints for roasting – thighs, legs or
    breasts, skin on
1 tablespoon mango chutney
small knob of softened butter
1 tablespoon Worcestershire sauce
1 tablespoon English mustard
pinch ground paprika
juice of half an orange
salt and freshly ground black pepper
1 tablespoon tomato ketchup

Put the chicken joints in a medium roasting tin, just large enough to hold them in an even layer. Mix together all the other ingredients, except the tomato ketchup, and spoon over the chicken.

Roast the chicken at 190C/375F/gas mark 5, basting frequently with the sauce, for about 45 minutes or until tender and quite charred on top. Lift the chicken from the pan juices and skim off any fat. Stir the tomato ketchup into the pan, taste the sauce for seasoning then spoon over the chicken before serving.

Chicken Escalopes Parmigiana
Serves 2

It was this simple dish of chicken baked in Parmesan crumbs that persuaded my four-year-old daughter to eat chicken. Keep the fillets whole or cut into bite-sized pieces. Either way, they're far better than chicken nuggets and great to make ahead and keep in the freezer.

    2 boneless, skinless chicken fillets
    50g/2oz fresh white breadcrumbs
    2 tablespoons grated Parmesan cheese
    1 small egg, beaten
    olive oil
    1 small aubergine, cut into cubes
    1 small onion, finely chopped
    1 small can chopped tomatoes
    knob of butter
    large pinch sugar
    small handful chopped fresh basil
    salt and freshly ground black pepper
    175g/6oz dried spaghetti

With a sharp knife split the chicken breasts from the plump side and open out like a book. Bat out lightly between two pieces of clingfilm (this may seem like a fiddle but it does cut down on the cooking time). Mix together the breadcrumbs and cheese. Dip the escalopes in the egg then into the crumb mixture. Pop the chicken in the fridge to chill while you make the pasta.

Heat a good drizzle of oil in a large saucepan and fry the aubergine with the onion over a high heat for about 10 minutes or until golden brown and soft. Add the tomatoes, butter, sugar and seasoning then simmer gently for 10 minutes. Stir in the basil.

Cook the spaghetti in a large pan of boiling water for about 10 minutes. While the spaghetti is cooking heat a drizzle of oil in a large frying pan and fry the crumbed chicken for about 4–5 minutes on each side until golden and crispy. Serve straight away with the aubergine sauce tossed through the spaghetti.

CHAPTER 3

Meat

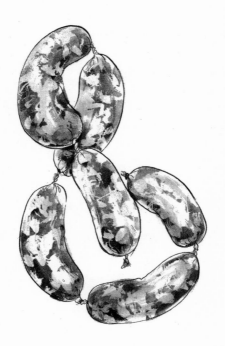

Hoisin and Honey Ribs
Serves 2

Pork spare ribs are excellent for cooking on the barbecue but shouldn't be kept just for summer. Children especially love getting sticky fingers! Use a mild honey, anything stronger will be too over-powering in flavour. Add whatever fruit juice you may have in the fridge. If you want to cook for four just double up the recipe.

450g/1lb pork spare ribs
75g hoisin sauce
1 tablespoon clear honey
1 teaspoon English mustard
2 teaspoons vinegar, distilled, white wine or cider
3 tablespoons tomato ketchup
2–3 tablespoons fruit juice, e.g. apple, orange or mango

To save on washing up, line a roasting tin with a double layer of foil and spread the spare ribs evenly over the base.

Whisk together all the remaining ingredients and spoon evenly over the ribs. At this stage it may look as though there is not enough liquid but the ribs will release a lot of fat as they cook. Cover the roasting tin with more foil and cook in the oven at 200C/400F/gas mark 6 for 30 minutes.

Uncover the ribs, turn them over in the cooking juices then return to the oven for a further 35–40 minutes or until dark golden brown, sticky and most of the liquid has evaporated. Baste the ribs occasionally as they cook. If the ribs are not colouring increase the oven temperature to 220C/425F/gas mark 7 for the final 10 minutes of cooking time. Serve immediately with a vegetable stir-fry.

Pork Chops with Apple and Fennel
Serves 2

I'm sure there are some who would consider a pork chop for supper an unimaginative choice but to me it's a delight. In summer I do very little with pork but cool autumn evenings demand 'bigger' suppers and the succulence and richness of this meat always feels just right.

Take one thickly cut chop of 'free-range' pork (with none of the fat removed please) and just one or two ingredients from the storecupboard and you can have a sumptuous supper within the magic 30 minutes. Whether it is fried with garlic, ginger and a squeeze of orange juice, bubbled with cream and mustard or grilled and topped with cheese, pork will rarely fail to please.

Fennel may not be the first flavouring that comes to mind when thinking of pork but I love its clean aniseed taste with the richness of the meat, especially a chop cooked till its fat is golden and juicy and crisp. Add some diced Bramley apple or pear and a lively apple juice to the pan and you have an instant 'sauce' to accompany it.

2 large, thick pork chops, about 225g/8oz each
salt and freshly ground black pepper
1 large Bramley (cooking) apple, peeled and chopped into
    smallish dice
2 large pinches fennel seeds
olive oil
2 garlic cloves, peeled and thinly sliced
about 25g/1oz butter
a generous wine glass of pure, unsweetened apple juice

With a sharp knife make several deep cuts through the rind and fat of the chops which will stop them curling up in the pan and help to crisp the fat. Rub the chops all over with salt and pepper, especially into the fat. Mix together the apple and fennel.

Heat a thin film of oil in a large frying pan and fry the garlic till golden and beginning to crisp. Add half the butter and leave the pan over the heat until the butter begins to foam a little then add the chops and the apple mixture. Leave the chops to spit and splutter undisturbed for 5 minutes by which time the underside should be golden and the apple beginning to soften and colour, then turn everything over. Leave it all to cook for another 4–5 minutes, occasionally pressing the fat of the pork down into the heat of the pan with the back of a wooden spoon. The apple should be soft and golden by now and the chops cooked through. The only reliable way to check and see is to cut into one of the chops with a sharp knife. It should look moist and creamy beige in the middle.

Remove the chops and any apple clinging to them to a hot plate. Pour the apple juice into whatever remains in the pan and keep the heat quite high. Scrape up the brown crusty bits from the bottom of the pan as the liquid begins to bubble. Take the pan off the heat and add the remaining butter. Swirl the pan around until the butter has just blended into the juices. Taste it; you may have to add more salt and pepper. Serve the chops straight away preferably with some fluffy mashed parsnips.

Pork Escalopes with a Goat's Cheese Crust
Serves 2

Just one day of warm spring sunshine can change my cooking overnight. Out go the slow-cooked hotpots, the roasts and braises and in come the grills and sautés, stir-fries, greens and salads.

This is a fast, mid-week supper of grilled pork that needs very little preparation. In fact it hardly needs a recipe, it's so simple. My butcher sells thinly sliced escalopes of pork and I have seen similar cuts in the supermarket. If you can't find them, pork chops or steaks are just as good but take a little longer to cook. If you have fresh sage in the garden add a couple of the leaves to the pork as it fries in the pan. Have some broccoli washed and ready to stir-fry, and put some small 'new' potatoes on to boil before you start to cook the pork.

> 4 thinly sliced pork escalopes
> olive oil
> butter
> 1½ slices white bread, processed into breadcrumbs
> about 50g/2oz mature Cheddar or Gruyère cheese, grated
> freshly ground black pepper
> 75g/3oz soft fresh goat's cheese, such as Chavroux

Put the escalopes between two sheets of clingfilm and bat out with a rolling pin or bottle. Make the pork as thin as you can as this cuts the cooking time and makes more space for the creamy goat's cheese topping. Season the escalopes with plenty of pepper.

Drizzle a little oil over the base of a large frying pan and add a small knob of butter. Heat together and when the butter starts to foam and sizzle add the pork escalopes and fry briskly for about 1 minute on each side or until they are golden brown (depending on the size of the escalopes you may have to fry them in batches). Add a little more oil and butter to the pan if it looks dry. Slide the escalopes onto a baking sheet.

Melt another knob of butter in the heat of the frying pan and stir it into the breadcrumbs with the grated cheese. Season with freshly ground black pepper.

Spread the goat's cheese very roughly over the pork. It really doesn't matter if it's quite thick in places. Sprinkle over the cheese and breadcrumb mixture and pop it under the hot grill quite close to the heat. Leave it there for about 3–4 minutes or until the top has turned a golden brown and is just starting to bubble. Eat immediately.

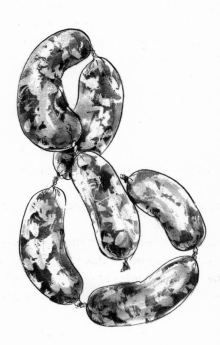

Pork Chops with Fresh Plums and Ginger
Serves 2

I've yet to find an imported plum worth eating, with the exception of the little French Mirabelle. Over the precious five or six weeks when our home-grown plums are in season I always tend to overbuy in fear of the day that I find they're gone for another year. But plums can be ripe and juicy one minute then turn to pulp the next, and this is the best use I have found yet for any fruit about to go over the top.

A pork chop browned in sizzling butter and oil then simmered with honey-sweet plums and ginger makes a sensational 30-minute supper. The pork needs to be thick and chunky with none of its creamy fat cut off. So buy traditionally-reared meat from the butcher. Most supermarkets are still obsessed with trimming and tend to offer chops that are too thinly cut for my taste.

2 chunky pork chops, about 200g/7oz each and about 1 inch
    thick
salt and freshly ground black pepper
2 tablespoons light soft brown sugar
a knob of fresh root ginger, peeled and finely grated
8 Victoria plums, halved and stoned
olive oil
butter
a wine glass of dry white wine

With a sharp knife make several deep cuts through the rind and fat of the chops, which will stop them curling up in the pan and help to crisp the fat. Rub the chops all over with salt and pepper especially into the fat. Stir the sugar and ginger into the plums.

Drizzle a thin film of oil over the base of a large frying pan and add a small knob of butter. Leave the pan over a moderate heat until the butter begins to foam a little, then add the chops. Leave them to spit and splutter undisturbed for 3–4 minutes, by which time the underside of the meat and the fat should be golden brown, then turn them over. Press the fat of the pork down into the heat of the pan with the back of a wooden spoon occasionally to help it brown.

After 1–2 minutes add the plums with any juice that has collected in the bowl and leave to cook with the chops for another 2–3 minutes until the chops are cooked through. The only reliable way to check and see is to cut into one of the chops with a sharp knife. It should look moist and creamy beige in the middle.

Remove the chops and most of the plums to a hot plate. Pour the wine into whatever remains in the pan and keep the heat quite high. Scrape up the brown crusty bits from the bottom of the pan as the liquid comes to the boil. Bubble for 3–4 minutes until the liquid has reduced by about half.

Take the pan off the heat and add another knob of butter about the size of a walnut in its shell. Swirl the pan around until the butter has just blended into the juices. Taste it, you may have to add a little more sugar (depending on the ripeness of the plums) and salt and pepper. Serve the chops and sauce straight away, preferably with some steamed couscous.

Pork Steaks with Sage and Apple
Serves 2

This is the fastest supper I know! It's based loosely (very loosely) on the Italian dish of Saltimbocca with veal, prosciutto, sage and wine.

> 2 slices pancetta (Italian bacon) or Parma ham
> 2 large pork shoulder steaks
> 2 large fresh sage leaves
> freshly ground black pepper
> olive oil
> 150ml/5fl oz pure, unsweetened apple juice or dry white
>   wine
> 50g/2oz chilled butter, diced
> squeeze of lemon juice

Lay a slice of pancetta or ham on top of each piece of pork with a fresh sage leaf and secure to the meat with a wooden cocktail stick. Season with a good grind of pepper.

Heat a drizzle of oil in a shallow frying pan and fry the pork for about 3–4 minutes on each side or until the pork is a good golden brown. Pour in the apple juice, which will sizzle and start to bubble immediately. Scrape the bottom of the pan with a wooden spoon to loosen any crusty bits and let the liquid bubble until only half is left. Lift the pork out onto a warm plate. Return the pan to the heat, add the butter and swirl it around. When it has melted into the pan juices, add a squeeze of lemon juice and pour over the pork before serving.

I've noticed ... thinly sliced pancetta, once only available in delis, is now in more and more supermarkets. You'll find it beside the pre-packed hams. It's an Italian bacon, which has a great flavour and is worth trying.

Pure, unsweetened apple juice ... makes a great substitute for white wine in many recipes if I don't have or want to use alcohol. There are plenty to choose from in all the supermarkets, but try to use a clear one with a sharp, clean flavour.

If you use ... a non-stick frying pan to brown the pork no extra oil is needed.

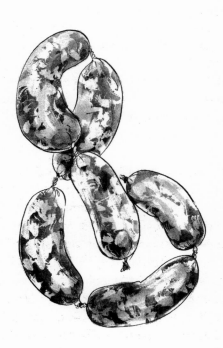

Grilled Lamb with Lemon
and Melting Onions
Serves 2

I love to grill lamb. Not only for the speed but also for the delicious crispy fat, the charred smoky flavour from the bits that start to blacken around the edges and the juiciness of the meat. I first cooked this spicy, aromatic lamb with chump chops but when I had to cook a half leg of lamb one night and there was no time to roast, I found that I preferred this version.

When the lamb is cooked with spices, onions, garlic and peppers alongside in the grill pan you get the most scrumptious, sweet sticky juices. Add some soft green salad leaves, a warm doughy bread and a pot of garlicky hummous to dollop on top for an absolute feast. Don't be surprised by the amount of salt. It helps to crisp the lamb fat and is offset by all the lemon juice.

about 350g/12oz diced leg lamb (don't be tempted to trim
   away all the fat)
1 medium onion, thinly sliced from tip to root
2 garlic cloves, peeled and sliced
1 red pepper, roughly chopped and seeded
½ teaspoon ground cumin
about ½ teaspoon salt and freshly ground black pepper
4 tablespoons olive oil
1 lemon

Put the lamb in a bowl with all the ingredients except the lemon. Toss it all together and set aside for at least 15 minutes, but ideally about 1 hour. Spread the lamb mixture in an even layer over the bottom of the grill pan. Halve the lemon and squeeze over the juice. Add the lemon halves to the pan too.

Heat the grill to its highest setting and place the pan about 5cm/2 inches away from the heat (some liquid will come out of the lamb and onions and this needs to evaporate away before the lamb will begin to brown so don't worry).

Turn the mixture over with a wooden spoon as it browns. After about 12–15 minutes the lamb should be pink in the middle and the onions and pepper soft. The flesh in the lemon halves will be soft and mellow now too.

Serve this with a big salad of floppy green leaves – oak leaf, baby spinach, soft round lettuce or a ready-washed bag of herb salad from the supermarket. I love the way the leaves start to wilt as they mix with the hot lamb juices on the plate. A hot doughy bread is good too. I've just discovered Khoubz in my local supermarket. It's a Middle Eastern style bread rather like a large round pitta. Heat them under the grill then wrap them in a tea towel to stop them becoming hard and crisp. Either fill with some of the salad and meat mixture or use to dip in the 'gravy'. A dollop of garlicky hummous works well too. If I have time I'll whiz it in the processor with a little of the grilled red pepper and a spoonful or two of crème fraîche or soured cream – whatever is in the fridge.

Braised Lamb Shanks with Harissa
Serves 2

I have a magical recipe for lamb shanks marinated then braised in Moroccan spices that I extracted from a reluctant chef many years ago. I enjoy cooking it occasionally for friends when I have the time to spend all day in the kitchen for it has a list of ingredients as long as my arm. This is my pared down supper version, simplified considerably for the sake of speed but a great supper none the less. It takes just 10–15 minutes to get it into the oven then just a lot of patience while it cooks. The aim is to braise the shanks until the meat is sweet and tender and falling off the bone, so the slower the better. You'll then be rewarded with a big-flavoured pot of aromatic lamb, mildly spiced in a rich tomato gravy. Hot, buttered couscous flecked with chopped fresh mint or coriander is, to my mind, the ideal accompaniment.

2 small lamb shanks
2 large onions, peeled and roughly chopped
1 medium aubergine, roughly chopped
olive oil
1 tablespoon harissa (Moroccan spice paste)
pared rind and juice of 1 large orange
1 glass red wine
350g jar tomato sauce such as Loyd Grossman's Primavera or
    Tomato & Basil or a 300ml pot chilled pasta sauce such as
    Napoletana or Arrabiatta
1 cinnamon stick
1 generous tablespoon honey

Preheat the oven to 170C/325F/gas mark 3. Put the lamb shanks, onion and aubergine in a large metal casserole and drizzle over a generous amount of olive oil. Put the casserole on the hob and stir everything over a high heat until the lamb is well browned on all sides and the onion beginning to colour and soften.

Lower the heat and add all the other ingredients. (Drop the squeezed orange halves into the pot too for extra flavour.) Pour in about 200ml/7fl oz water. The liquid should come about half way up the shanks. Bring the liquid to the boil then cover the casserole tightly and simmer in the low oven for about 2½ hours. Test the lamb with a fork: it should be so tender it almost falls off the bone. If the sauce looks too thin remove the lamb and bubble the sauce on the hob until it has reduced and thickened a little.

If you're planning ahead . . . cook the lamb shanks one night and reheat and serve the next. Remove the cinnamon stick when the lamb is cooked otherwise I've found that its flavour becomes too overpowering.

Finally . . . any leftover lamb can be roughly shredded and stirred through the spicy tomato sauce. It makes a great mixture to toss into hot pasta for supper the following night.

Grilled Gammon with Spice
Rub and Mango Mojo
Serves 2

Mango mojo is a fresh, uncooked chutney that could easily partner any grilled meat or curries. I love its sweet spiciness with the slightly salty gammon. I've used two mangoes, as one is just never enough and any leftovers can be kept, covered, in the fridge. The chilli adds a little heat and a splash of colour but can be omitted if not everyone likes it.

large pinch ground cumin
large pinch ground paprika
1 teaspoon soft brown sugar
2 tablespoons olive oil
2 smoked gammon steaks, about 225g/8oz each

For the Mango Mojo
2 large ripe mangoes
juice of 2 limes
½ fresh red chilli, de-seeded and chopped
1 handful fresh coriander, finely chopped
pinch soft brown sugar

Mix together the spices, sugar and olive oil to make a smooth paste. Put the gammon steaks on a foil-lined grill rack and brush or spread the spice rub over both sides. Preheat the grill on its highest setting.

To make the mango mojo, peel and remove the flesh from the mango. Neatly dice one slice of flesh and set aside. Purée the remaining mango with the lime juice then stir in the chilli, coriander and diced mango. Taste the sauce and add a little brown sugar to taste.

Grill the gammon steaks for about 5 minutes on each side,

basting with the cooking juices once or twice. Serving immediately with the mango mojo.

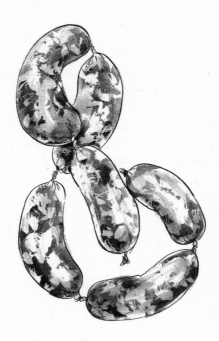

Butterfly Lamb with Onion & Cumin
Serves 2

Souvlakia, the Greek dish of tender, chargrilled lamb eaten wrapped in wafer thin bread, was the inspiration for this supper. I first encountered it in an open-air cinema in Skiathos where we sat clutching these hot spicy parcels waiting for the sun to go down and the evening's film to begin. I've used the same simple marinade of onions, cumin and garlic but on 'butterflied' lamb. This is a half leg of lamb, boned and opened out so that it can lie almost flat in a roasting tin. Any butcher will do this for you. You'll find that the lamb will cook in almost half the time giving wonderful crispy fat and juicy pink meat that can then be cut into thick slices for serving.

Two or three spoonfuls of natural yoghurt stirred into the roasting juices make the perfect sauce.

1 large Spanish onion, roughly chopped
1 teaspoon cumin seeds
3 fat garlic cloves
large pinch cayenne pepper
salt and freshly ground black pepper
olive oil
half leg of lamb, boned and opened out flat
10–12 small new potatoes, scrubbed
2–3 tablespoons natural yoghurt (a creamy, pouring one)

Preheat the oven to 230C/450F/gas mark 8. Whiz the onion, cumin, garlic and cayenne pepper in a food processor with 1 teaspoon ground black pepper and 6 tablespoons of olive oil until reduced to a thick sludge.

Put the lamb in a non-metallic dish and spoon over the onion mixture. Rub it well into the fleshy side of the meat then cover and leave to marinate for as long as you can. Overnight is ideal but 30 minutes is better than nothing at all.

Scrape the marinade off the lamb and put the meat skin side up in a roasting tin just large enough to hold the lamb comfortably. If it's too big the lamb juices will evaporate away but if it's too small the lamb will just stew.

Put the potatoes into the marinade left in the dish; stir them around then spoon evenly around the lamb with any of the remaining onion mixture. Season everything with salt and add a little more olive oil, just enough to leave a thin layer over the base of the roasting tin.

Roast the lamb for 30 minutes, then reduce the heat to 180C/350F/gas mark 4 for a further 20–25 minutes or until the lamb and potatoes are both golden and tender. Check the pan juices when lowering the oven temperature, and if the pan looks too dry add another drizzle of oil or 2–3 tablespoons of water.

Remove the lamb to a chopping board for slicing and spoon the potatoes into a serving dish to keep warm. With the roasting tin off the heat, stir the yoghurt into the pan juices scraping up all the caramelized onion from the bottom. Taste for seasoning (it will probably need a little salt) then serve just warm with the thickly sliced lamb and potatoes.

Try . . .

• The marinated lamb without the potatoes is perfect for cooking on the barbecue. Wait until the coals have died down a little to a moderate heat, then allow the lamb 30–35 minutes on the coals. Roast the potatoes in the oven separately.

Red Lamb and Pumpkin Coconut Curry
Serves 2

All good cookery books will tell you that Thai curry paste, like pesto, is much better when fresh and homemade. They will also tell you that it's a doddle to make. All this is perfectly true but only if you have all the ingredients to hand. If, like me, you occasionally yearn for the fragrant spiciness of a Thai curry but always seem to have at least one or two of the essential ingredients missing, try this simplified version. It may not be strictly authentic but it produces a delectably aromatic supper. Ten to fifteen minutes preparation is all that is needed to get this curry cooking, leaving you around an hour to enjoy a glass of wine or do other things. I have included a recipe for a home-made curry paste if you want to plan ahead and buy all the necessary ingredients. Once made it will keep for up to a week in a screw-top jar in the fridge (I don't freeze the paste as I think it loses too much of its freshness).

> 350g/12oz leg of lamb
> a light oil such as grape seed or groundnut
> 1 large red onion, chopped
> 125g/4oz block creamed coconut, roughly chopped
> 1 teaspoon Thai red curry paste (see page 87)
> large knob fresh root ginger, peeled and finely grated
> 1 garlic clove, crushed
> 175g/6oz pumpkin, cut into chunky wedges
> 30ml/2 level tablespoons mango chutney
> a handful of fresh coriander leaves

Cut the lamb into large pieces just slightly bigger than one mouthful. Heat a little oil in a deep pan and when it starts to sizzle fry the lamb, a few pieces at a time, until it turns a deep golden brown all over. Remove with a slotted spoon then add the onion to the pan with an extra drizzle of oil if it looks dry. Fry, stirring in any crusty bits remaining from the lamb, until the onion is soft and golden. Take a good 10 minutes to do this as it brings out the natural 'sweetness' of the onions and adds to both the flavour and colour of the finished curry.

While the onions are cooking pour ½ pint of boiling water over the creamed coconut and leave to dissolve.

Return the lamb to the pan with the curry paste, ginger and garlic then fry everything together for about 2 minutes or until the lamb is evenly coated in the spice mixture. Stir in the coconut liquid and bring to the boil then cover the pan and simmer very gently for 30 minutes.

Stir the pumpkin and chutney into the lamb, cover again and continue to cook for a further 30 minutes or until the lamb and pumpkin are very tender. Stir a handful of coriander leaves into the curry just before serving over some Thai or basmati rice.

Shredded Pork Wraps
Serves 4

This may sound a little unusual but it is a good way of cooking pork tenderloin. It's the perfect dish for those evenings when supper is on the run and everyone seems to want to eat at different times. Plus, most of the ingredients you will probably have on hand. Cook the pork and let everyone make up their own wraps when they want them. Alternatively use to top baked potatoes or fill ciabatta rolls.

1 large onion, finely chopped
1 garlic clove, crushed
2 tablespoons olive oil
2 tablespoons cider or white wine vinegar
150ml/5fl oz tomato ketchup
2 teaspoons Worcestershire sauce
150ml/5fl oz apple juice
2 tablespoons mango or other fruit chutney
salt and freshly ground black pepper
1 pork fillet

To serve:
Mediterranean wrap 'breads'
mixed salad and couscous

In a deep flameproof casserole cook the onion and garlic in the oil until very soft and golden. Stir in all the remaining ingredients except the pork. Bring to the boil then simmer gently for 10 minutes. Drop in the pork, cover tightly and continue to simmer gently on the hob or in a low oven, 170C/325F/gas mark 3, for 45 minutes or until the pork is very tender and falls apart easily when pierced with a fork. Shred the pork into large, bite-sized pieces using two forks. Taste the sauce for seasoning.

Open out the wraps and spoon on some couscous and salad.
Spoon on a little of the shredded pork and sauce then wrap up
and eat straight away.

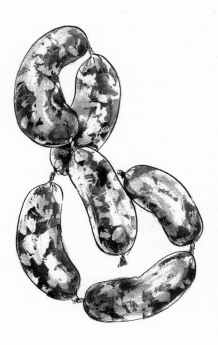

Roast Rack of Lamb with Yoghurt and Spices
Serves 2

A rack of lamb will rarely let you down. As a weekday supper, it may be more expensive than chops but I think it's worth every penny. Such a neat little package with its six or seven cutlets, it's just the perfect roast for two. It promises tender, sweet meat and (best of all) plenty of charred and smoky bones to chew. I sometimes pop one into the oven with just a lick of Dijon mustard and olive oil and it always emerges tender and delicious.

Good butchers will always be happy to prepare a rack and many supermarkets now stock them too although most cut away far too much of the creamy fat for my taste.

If you want to plan ahead, the spiced onion and yoghurt mixture can be made the day before.

1 teaspoon cumin seeds
1 teaspoon mustard seeds
1 teaspoon coriander seeds
1 large onion, very finely chopped
olive oil
pinch cayenne pepper
salt and freshly ground black pepper
small tub natural yoghurt (a set bio yoghurt is best)
a rack of lamb with about 6 or 7 bones.

Tip the spice seeds into a dry frying pan and place over a low to medium heat and cook for a minute or two until they start to pop and you can smell their fragrance. Put them in a spice mill, coffee grinder or pestle and mortar and grind to a rough powder (if you have none of the above put the spices on a board and crush them with the base of a heavy pan). Put the onion in the frying pan and drizzle over a little olive oil. Cook the onion over a moderate heat until it is soft and translucent, about 6–7 minutes, then stir in all the spices. Stir over the heat for another 2–3 minutes without colouring the onion, then take the pan off the heat and leave the mixture to cool down.

Beat the yoghurt in its pot until it becomes thin and creamy then stir it into the spiced onions with plenty of salt and pepper.

Put the lamb in a shallow roasting tin, season generously with salt then put it in a hot oven, 230C/450F/gas mark 8 for 15 minutes. Remove and spread the yoghurt mix all over the meat, both flesh and fat. Return the lamb to the oven and continue cooking until it is to your liking, probably another 15 minutes for a pink roast.

Switch the oven off and leave the door ajar for 5 minutes. This will give the lamb a few minutes to rest and make it easier to cut into chops. Serve them with a bright, fresh relish of mango and mint, see page 86.

Mango and Mint Relish

1 small ripe mango
1 to 2 tablespoons natural yoghurt
2 tablespoons chopped fresh mint
squeeze of lemon juice
salt

Peel and cube the mango. Beat the yoghurt until it is fairly smooth then stir into the mango with the mint, lemon juice and salt.

Thai Red Curry Paste

1 teaspoon cumin seeds
2 teaspoons coriander seeds
groundnut oil
6–8 large red chillis, de-seeded and chopped
3 stalks lemon grass, peeled down to the tender heart and
    chopped
a large handful coriander leaves
a long finger of fresh root ginger (or galangal), peeled and
    chopped
3 shallots, finely chopped
4 garlic cloves
grated rind and juice of 1 large lime
1 teaspoon coarsely ground black peppercorns

Fry the seeds in a little hot oil until they begin to sizzle in the
pan. Leave to cool a little while you put all the remaining ingredients in a blender. Add the fried spices and whiz everything
together to a paste. You may need to scrape the mixture down
the sides of the blender occasionally and add a little extra lime
juice or water until everything is mashed to a paste. Pot, cover
and store in the fridge.

Slow-cooked Lamb with Oranges and Sherry Vinegar

Serves 4

I have been making this recipe for years and never tire of it with its golden, saffron-rich juices and tang of oranges and spices. Around Christmas time it's ideal, when most of us are trying to cram too much into the day and there's often little time left to prepare supper. Just throw all the ingredients into the sherry overnight, then into a pot to simmer in the oven for an hour or so. It also freezes like a dream so I tend to double up and keep batches in store for those evenings when I rush in and just want to get supper on the table with no fuss.

I've given ingredients for four servings, as it would be silly to make this for any less, so invite some friends round or cool and freeze the leftovers. If you're going to use boned shoulder of lamb, ask the butcher to slice it thickly for you then cut it into pieces about two bites in size. I tend to avoid ready-diced lamb as it is invariably cut too small and so shrinks to horrid little lumps once cooked.

700g/1½lbs boned shoulder of lamb, cut into large pieces
1 teaspoon ground cumin
large pinch ground cloves
1 teaspoon dried thyme
3 fat garlic cloves, crushed
100ml/4fl oz fresh orange juice
75g/3oz kumquats
about 25g/1oz raisins
1 teaspoon saffron threads
150ml/5fl oz medium sherry
3 tablespoons vinegar, preferably sherry or white wine
olive oil
2 scant tablespoons flour

300ml/½ pint stock
salt and freshly ground black pepper

Put the lamb in a glass or china bowl with the cumin, cloves, thyme, garlic, orange juice, whole kumquats, raisins, saffron, sherry, vinegar and about 1 tablespoon of olive oil. Cover and set aside overnight, somewhere cool but not necessarily the fridge.

Preheat the oven to 180C/350F/gas mark 4. Lift the lamb from the marinade and pat dry with kitchen paper. Heat a good drizzle of olive oil in a medium-sized casserole, one to which you have a lid. When it starts to sizzle, add a few pieces of lamb and leave them in the hot oil for a minute or two to brown on one side. Turn the pieces over and brown the other side. Repeat with the remaining lamb. Getting a good colour on the lamb ensures that the finished cooking juices will be rich and dark so it's worth taking a bit of extra time at this stage.

Return all the meat to the pan and stir in the flour. Keep stirring over the heat until the flour has turned golden brown, then pour in the marinade liquid and the soaked fruits. Add the stock now with plenty of salt and pepper and bring the liquid to the boil.

Cover the casserole with the lid, then put it in the oven to simmer for about 1 hour or until the meat is very tender. Taste the juices, you may need to add a little salt, then serve hot with some pilau rice and a salad.

Herby Lamb with Avocado Hummous
Serves 2–3

The lamb does benefit, both in flavour and texture, from being left overnight in the yoghurt marinade. Ask your butcher to 'butterfly' the lamb for you and the rest is easy.

    1 small half leg of lamb, boned
    1 large bunch mint, roughly chopped
    1 large bunch fresh coriander, roughly chopped
    3 garlic cloves, peeled
    225g/8oz natural yoghurt
    sea salt and freshly ground black pepper
    175g/6oz hummous
    1 ripe avocado
    juice of ½ lemon

Open out the lamb so that it will lie flat on the work surface. Make extra cuts if necessary to allow you to open it out to an even thickness. Most butchers will happily do this for you. Slash the fat side of the lamb and season well.

Put the coriander, mint and garlic in a food processor and whiz together until roughly chopped. Add the yoghurt and seasoning.

Put the lamb into a non-metallic dish and spoon over half the marinade. Rub the mixture into the lamb then cover and put it in the fridge overnight.

To cook, take the lamb out of the dish and place it in a roasting tin. Roast at 200C/425F/gas mark 7 for about 30–40 minutes or until blackened on the outside and pink in the middle. If barbecuing, start the meat off in the oven for 20 minutes then finish over the barbecue coals for a further 20 minutes.

While the lamb is cooking, mash the hummous and avocado

flesh into the remaining marinade. Spoon into a dish and squeeze over the lemon juice. When ready to serve, stir the avocado hummous to mix in the lemon juice and taste for seasoning. Serve with the thickly sliced lamb and a tomato, onion and Feta cheese salad.

Pan-fried Liver with Marsala and Onions
Serves 2

When the days get warmer and the evenings lighter, I'm often guilty of staying out too long in the garden. So supper is sometimes a very rushed affair indeed. The most useful thing to have in the fridge for such evenings is liver, for the quicker it's cooked the better. In fact the worse thing that you can do to liver is overcook it. Just a few seconds too long and its velvety texture suddenly turns to dried rubber. Now, how you like your liver is a personal thing. I don't like the fashion for serving it rare but do think that it's best eaten when it's more pink than brown inside.

This simple supper of pan-fried liver with Marsala and vinegar is utterly delicious and unbelievably simple. It's based on a classic Sicilian recipe and I've added the onions for I just can't imagine liver without them. As an additional side dish a creamy mash of sweet potatoes, with a little orange rind or juice, is hard to beat plus a salad of soft green leaves. But whatever you decide to serve with the liver, have it all cooked and ready before you start frying for once the liver hits the pan you won't have time to do anything else.

olive oil
about 50g/2oz butter
2 large Spanish onions, sliced
225g/8oz lamb's liver, thinly sliced
6 tablespoons Marsala, Madeira or medium sherry
1 tablespoon red wine vinegar
salt and freshly ground black pepper

Drizzle some olive oil into a large frying pan, just enough to cover the base. Add a small knob of the butter, about the size of a sugar cube, and stir in the onions. Leave them to cook over a low to moderate heat for a good 15 minutes until they are soft, deep golden brown and caramelized a little. It's worth taking the time at this stage to get the onions very soft. Don't be tempted to stir them too often as this stops them colouring. If I have the time I sometimes put the onions with the oil and butter into a small roasting tin and brown them slowly in a moderate oven for about 30 minutes.

Remove the softened onions to a plate and add another drizzle of oil and small knob of butter to the pan (no need to wipe it out). When the butter starts to sizzle and splutter add the liver. Leave the slices undisturbed for about 1 minute, which allows them to brown underneath, then flip them over and brown the other side for 1 minute. Remove the liver and pop it on top of the onions. It will still look bloody at this stage but don't worry.

Stir the Marsala and vinegar into the pan; it will bubble up immediately. As it does, scrape up the brown sticky bits from the bottom. Add the remaining butter and keep the sauce gently bubbling until it has all blended into the liquid. Taste for seasoning then return the liver and onions to the pan. Stir over the heat for barely a minute to heat through and finish cooking the liver, then eat immediately.

Pan-fried Steak
Serves 2

Steak is one of the simplest of suppers. Although I don't cook it very often, I do occasionally long for its charred, meaty flavour. To be good, really good, I believe a steak must be pan-fried or griddled until it is crusty and almost blackened on the outside but still pink and juicy within. It needs nothing more than some form of potatoes, either boiled floury ones in their skins, fat crispy chips or salty sautés. I always buy steak from my local butcher who sells well-hung meat that's tender and full of flavour. His steaks are dark, ruby red in colour with a good marbling of creamy fat.

    2 x 200g/7oz sirloin or rump steaks
    olive oil
    salt and freshly ground black pepper
    Leek and Mustard Butter Sauce to accompany

Rub the steaks all over with a little olive oil and pepper then get a frying pan or cast iron grill pan very hot. Leave it on the hob for a good three or four minutes until you can feel the heat above the pan then drop on the steaks. Leave them alone for at least 2 minutes to give them time to seal and form a crisp crust on the underside, then turn them over and season with salt.

It's virtually impossible to give exact timings for steaks as so much depends on the size, quality and thickness of the meat and your own taste. As a very rough guide about 2–3 minutes either side will produce rare steaks and 3–4 minutes medium rare. Get into the habit of feeling the cooking meat instead and you'll soon get to know when a steak's done to your liking. As a general rule, if the steak is still soft to the touch it's rare. If it gives some resistance it's pink rather than red in the middle and if it feels quite firm it's well done.

Serve the steak the moment it's ready with some warm Leek and Mustard Butter Sauce, see page 96.

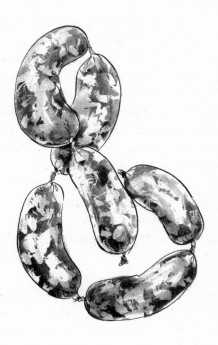

Leek and Mustard Butter Sauce
Serves 2

During the winter I buy leeks almost every week, I love their subtle flavour and versatility. This mellow and piquant butter sauce, loosely based on the classic Béarnaise, is perfect with steak and worth every second of stirring and beating. It's also excellent with a roast rib of beef. Make the sauce first; it will wait while you cook the steak.

  half a small leek, about 125g/4oz, finely diced
  125g/4oz butter, cut into small cubes
  4 tablespoons white wine vinegar
  plenty of freshly ground black pepper, about ½ teaspoon
  2 large egg yolks
  1 tablespoon Dijon mustard
  small handful chopped fresh parsley, if you have it

Put the leek in a sieve and rinse it under cold water to wash away any grit. Heat just a knob of the butter in a small saucepan and add the leek with the water that's still clinging to it. Cook the leek over a moderate heat, stirring occasionally, until it is completely soft. This will take a good 10 minutes but as it's the main ingredient of the sauce, it's worth taking some care.

When the leek is soft, add the vinegar and pepper with 2 tablespoons water. Bring to the boil and bubble until there is virtually no liquid left, just enough to coat the leek. This will only take a minute or two. Set aside.

Put the egg yolks in a heatproof bowl and beat in the mustard with a wooden spoon. Set the bowl over a pan of gently bubbling water, making sure that the bottom of the bowl is just hovering above the water level. Add the butter a little at a time, stirring constantly over the heat until it has blended into the egg. With each addition of butter the sauce will thicken until it looks creamy, like soft mayonnaise. Stir in the leek. It may at this stage show signs of going grainy but beat quickly for a few seconds and it will come back together. Taste the sauce; it may need a little salt.

The sauce will keep warm sitting over the hot water (off the heat) while you cook the steak. If it looks grainy again, a spoonful of boiling water beaten in will bring it back.

For an alternative sauce . . . remove the cooked steak from the pan and keep warm. Pour a glass of red wine or sherry into the pan and bubble it for 2–3 minutes, scraping any bits of browned meat from the bottom of the pan. Swirl in a small knob of butter then season and spoon over the steak.

Steak with Sugared Onions,
Mustard and Beer
Serves 2

There is no great mystique to cooking the perfect steak – all it takes is some good beef and a hot pan. And by 'good beef' I mean of course British beef. A well-hung sirloin or rump steak would always be my first choice, fried till the fat is crisp and golden and the meat juicy pink inside. Add a simple sauce of caramelized onions and lager and you have (probably) the best steak supper in the world.

olive oil
a large knob of butter
1 large red onion, cut in half then into thick segments
about 2 teaspoons Demerara or light Muscovado sugar
2 thick rump or sirloin steaks, as large as you like
salt and freshly ground black pepper
50ml/2fl oz stock
150ml/¼ pint lager
small pinch dried thyme if you have it
1 tablespoon Dijon mustard

Drizzle a little oil over the base of a heavy frying pan and add the butter. Place over a moderate heat and when the butter begins to bubble and splutter, add the onions and cook until they soften and turn a rich golden brown without burning. This will take a good 10–12 minutes. Increase the heat under the pan, stir in the sugar and cook for a few minutes until it has melted through the onions. Remove them and set aside.

Rub the steaks all over with a little olive oil and plenty of pepper then get the frying pan very hot. Leave it on the hob for a good three or four minutes until you can feel the heat above it then drop in the steaks. Leave them alone for at least 2 minutes to give them time to seal and form a dark golden crust on the underside then turn them over. It's always better to feel the cooking meat instead of timing it. You'll soon get to know when a steak's done to your liking. As a general rule, if the steak is still soft to the touch it's rare. If a finger pressed into the top leaves a slight indentation it's pink rather than red in the middle and if it feels quite firm it's well done. If in doubt cut into the meat with a sharp knife to check. The meat will release some of its juices but as the sauce in this recipe is made in the same pan nothing will be lost. Remove the steaks to a warmed ovenproof dish and cover with foil to keep hot.

Stir the stock and lager into the hot pan and bring to the boil, stirring in any browned bits left from the steaks. Turn down the heat again, return the onions and add the thyme if you're using it. Leave the sauce to bubble gently until it looks reduced by about half and a little syrupy. Stir in the mustard, taste for seasoning and serve immediately with the hot steaks.

Saturday Night Supper
Serves 2

Don't let the long cooking time put you off making this braised beef. It's prepared and in the oven in just 15 minutes and virtually looks after itself. Like so many slow-cooked foods, the beef tastes even better the next day so it has become a favourite one-pot supper to cook ahead on a Friday night for a lazy Saturday night in.

Although my husband doesn't like anchovies, he loves this beef because the fillets melt into the cooking juices and blend with the capers and mustard to produce a delicious piquant flavour.

about 2 or 3 tablespoons olive oil
1 large Spanish onion, cut into thin wedges from tip to root
450g/1lb braising steak, cut into small 'steaks' (larger than
    one mouthful)
1 small can anchovy fillets in oil, drained and chopped
2 tablespoons capers, rinsed well and roughly chopped
a palmful of chopped fresh mixed parsley and thyme
1 generous teaspoon ready-made English mustard

Preheat the oven to 170C/325F/gas mark 3. Heat about 1 tablespoon of oil in a small flameproof casserole, one to which you have a lid. Stir in the onion and cook over a medium heat for 3–4 minutes until golden and translucent then remove with a draining spoon.

Heat a little more oil in the pan, then brown the meat just 2 or 3 pieces at a time (any more than that and the meat tends to stew rather than brown). To get a good colour on the meat leave the pieces sizzling in the oil for a minute or two without moving them then turn the meat over and brown the other side. When the last of the meat has been browned pour 4 tablespoons cold water into the pan and scrape up any crusty bits from the bottom with a wooden spoon.

Put the onion back into the pan with all the other ingredients and toss everything together with your hands.

Crumple a large sheet of greaseproof paper and hold it under the cold tap until completely wet. Shake off any excess water, open out the paper and press it down over the top of the beef mixture. Cover with the lid to keep in the moisture and cook for about 1½–2 hours. Check the pot after 1 hour to make sure that it's still moist. Add a little extra water if the pan looks dry. When the beef is meltingly tender taste for seasoning, it might need a bit of pepper, then serve.

If cooked the night before . . . reheat the beef by adding about 50ml/2fl oz water to the pan and simmer it gently on the hob without too much stirring for 10–15 minutes or until it's piping hot.

Slow-cooked Oxtail with Pepper, Thyme and Orange
Serves 2

Along with Arbroath smokies, my mother's tattie and leek soup and any cheese you might mention, oxtail is one of my 'desert island' foods. I love it sweet, succulent and falling off the bone in a rich, dark braise with winter roots, orange and red wine. But when I found some at the back of the freezer I thought I'd try cooking it like Italian Ossobuco – the Milanese braised shin of veal that is cooked with white wine, celery, orange and gutsy herbs – and I liked the results. Serve it with chunks of warm ciabatta bread or a bowl of fragrant saffron rice into which you have tossed some chopped fresh parsley and lemon rind.

It does have a longer list of ingredients than I would normally want to use but it's incredibly simple to make and is best cooked one night ready to reheat and serve the next.

1 oxtail, jointed
flour for dusting
olive oil
butter
1 large Spanish onion, finely chopped
2 garlic cloves, peeled
small bunch fresh thyme, tied with fine string
2 sticks celery, finely chopped
1 red pepper, halved, de-seeded and finely chopped
300ml/½ pint dry white wine
300ml/½ pint vegetable stock
salt and freshly ground black pepper
rind and juice of 1 large orange

Preheat the oven to 170C/325F/gas mark 3. Dust the oxtail lightly with flour. Heat a drizzle of oil in a casserole and melt a knob of butter in it. Add the oxtail pieces and fry them over a high heat until a dark brown on all sides. They should sizzle and splutter in the pan if it's hot enough. The darker the colour of the oxtail at this stage, the better the colour and flavour of the final cooking juices.

Remove the oxtail, lower the heat then stir in the onion, whole garlic cloves, thyme bundle, celery and red pepper. There should be enough fat left in the pan to cook these but if not add a little more oil. Cook, stirring, until golden, translucent and starting to soften.

Add the wine, stock and seasoning and bring to the boil, then cover and cook in the low oven for two hours. Cool the oxtail then cover and keep overnight in the fridge. When ready to use the next evening, skim off any fat that has set on the surface then bring the oxtail to the boil, add the pared rind and juice of the orange and return to a low oven for a further 1 hour or until the meat is very tender and falling off the bone.

Serve hot in deep bowls or soup plates with chunks of bread or saffron rice.

Oxtail for a Cold
January Day
Serves 2

It's that time of year again: everyone I know is on a diet. Some are de-toxing on a regime of no carbohydrates, others are eating copious quantities of cabbage soup and I have a husband trying to get trim for skiing. 'Forget it', I say. When it turns cold and frosty all I want is some real food. By this I mean a proper fish pie, a bowl of tattie and leek soup or perhaps an aromatic pot of oxtail that has been simmering for hours in the oven.

Although this supper takes time to cook I still think of it as being an easy option. For once everything is chopped and browned it will sit happily in the oven for about for 2–3 hours while I get on with something else. It's a meal-in-a-bowl type of supper that should be spooned into warm soup plates and served with a generous chunk of bread.

Don't use any old plonk and hope that it will be OK: it won't. I always buy a hefty red and make sure it's one I'll be happy to drink while I cook.

If oxtail doesn't appeal, the same recipe can be used with 2 large lamb leg steaks.

1 oxtail
flour for dusting
olive oil
2 small onions, peeled
2 fat garlic cloves
2 sticks celery, roughly chopped
a large knob of fresh root ginger, peeled and thinly sliced
a bottle of gutsy red red wine
salt and freshly ground black pepper
pared rind and juice of 1 orange
a generous tablespoon clear honey

1 large sweet potato, peeled and cut into very large chunks
   (about two mouthfuls)

Preheat the oven to 170C/325F/gas mark 3. Dust the oxtail lightly with flour. Heat a drizzle of oil in a casserole and add the oxtail pieces. Fry them over a high heat until a dark brown on all sides. They will sizzle and splutter in the pan if it's hot enough. The darker the colour of the oxtail at this stage, the better.

Remove the oxtail, lower the heat, then stir in the onion, whole garlic cloves, celery and ginger. There should be enough fat left in the pan to cook these but if not add a touch more oil. Cook, stirring, until the onions are golden, translucent and beginning to soften. Pour yourself a generous glass of red wine then add the reminder to the casserole with a good grinding of salt and pepper.

Bring to the boil then cover and cook in the low oven for 1½–2 hours. Add the pared rind and juice of the orange with the honey and sweet potato and return to a low oven for a further 1 hour or until the meat is very tender and falling off the bone.

Serve hot in deep bowls or soup plates with chunks of bread.

Stovies
Serves 2

If you can save the crunchy little bits of beef and the rich, jellied brown gunge lying on the bottom of the roasting tin from being nibbled or cleared away after Sunday lunch transform them with the beef dripping, some tatties and onion into a blissful supper for a cold Monday night – stovies.

To me, stovies (stoved potatoes) is the ultimate Scottish comfort food. It always brings back memories of energetic ceilidhs where a welcome plate of stovies would be served to sustain us well into the night. There are endless variations. My mother always cooks hers slowly on the hob with just the dripping, while I prefer to simmer mine slowly in the oven with a little stock and to remove the lid for the last 10 minutes so that the potatoes are crisp on top and soft and savoury underneath.

A pot of stovies can be prepared and ready for the oven in just 15 minutes and cooks pretty much all by itself so I always consider it an easy supper. Most varieties of potatoes, whether they're waxy or mealy, will be fine to use. Having said that, floury Maris Pipers are a particularly favourite of mine for this.

3 large potatoes
about 125g/4oz cold roast beef, including all the over-
    cooked, little crusty bits from the roasting tin
2–3 tablespoons beef dripping (if you have no dripping use
    butter rather than oil)
4 medium size onions, thinly sliced
leftover gravy and meat juices or beef stock
salt and freshly ground black pepper

Preheat the oven to 190C/375F/gas mark 5. Scrub the potatoes and remove any nasties but don't bother to peel them unless you really want to. Roughly shred the beef.

Warm the dripping in a deep, ovenproof pot until it melts then add the onions. Cook them over a moderate heat until they're beginning to soften and turn a pale golden brown. This will take about 10 minutes, stirring the onions from time to time.

Thinly slice the potatoes into the pan and add the shredded beef with about 8 tablespoons of gravy, meat juices or stock. Season generously with salt and pepper then stir everything together with a wooden spoon to mix the onion and beef through the potatoes.

Cover the pan with a tight-fitting lid and pop it in the oven for about 40 minutes or until the potatoes are meltingly soft.

Remove the lid, stir the stovies (I like it if the bottom layer has stuck and browned a little) and taste the potato. Add more salt and pepper now if it needs it. Increase the oven temperature to 220/425F/gas mark 7 and return the stovies for another 10–15 minutes or until the top turns golden brown and crisp.

If you need an extra vegetable ... fry some coarsely shredded Savoy cabbage (the dark crinkly one) in a little butter with a splash of water until it just begins to soften. Season and add a squeeze of lemon juice just before serving.

Summer Meat Loaf with Roasted Peppers and Garlic

Fills a 900g/2lb loaf tin

I love to see the fat, pink-tinged bulbs of fresh garlic arrive in my greengrocers. The big cloves, juicy and mild, are easily slipped from their skins and have a wonderful, crisp and crunchy texture. Make the most of them for within a month they'll begin to dry out again. When roasted with red peppers and olive oil, fresh garlic turns golden and buttery and almost sweet with caramelized juices – just perfect for studding through a summer meat loaf.

Traditional meat loaf has fallen from fashion recently in favour of more stylish terrines and patés but I think there are few things more useful to have in the fridge come summer. You can serve it with crusty bread and pickles for lunch, or pack it for a picnic. I can't resist it warm from the oven with homemade potato salad and some summer greens for supper. Or just break off a mouthful as you're passing the fridge.

a head of fresh garlic
3 large red peppers
extra virgin olive oil
450g/1lb minced beef
125g/4oz minced pork
125g/4oz fatty salami or saucisson, finely chopped
2 eggs
salt and freshly ground black pepper
handful fresh parsley, finely chopped
about 50g/2oz Roquefort, St Agur or other soft, blue-veined
    cheese, crumbled

Break the garlic bulb into individual cloves but don't peel them. Throw them into a shallow roasting tin with the whole peppers and drizzle everything with a little oil. Roast at 200C/400F/gas mark 6 for about 20–25 minutes or until the pepper skins are blackened and wrinkled and the garlic golden.

Leave the peppers for 3–4 minutes until they are cool enough to handle, then peel off the skin. Halve each pepper then scrape out and discard the core and seeds. Cut the flesh into dice about the size of the garlic cloves. Pop the garlic from its skin, then halve each clove. Stir the garlic with the pepper back into any juices in the roasting tin.

Put all the remaining ingredients, except the cheese, into a large bowl and mix together by hand until everything is thoroughly combined. You could do this in a food processor but I find that the mixture becomes over-processed too quickly.

Add the crumbled cheese, diced peppers, garlic pieces and any juices from the roasting tin, then mix lightly through the meat mixture. Spoon into a lightly oiled 900g/2lb loaf tin and cook, uncovered, in the oven at 190C/375F/gas mark 5 for about 1 hour 15 minutes. Pour off any juices and cool. Serve warm in thick slices or chill overnight in the fridge before using.

Toad-in-the-Hole
Serves 2

I've just rediscovered the joy of toad-in-the-hole. I haven't eaten it since my schooldays but when I needed to turn a few sausages and a bit of bacon into something comforting on a wet and windy evening I suddenly hankered after this rib-sticker. The real joy of this simple (and cheap) dish lies in the contrast between the crispy batter on top and the soft savoury middle. I've stuck pretty closely to the traditional recipe except to brown the sausages first (I hate grey sausages) and to add a little smoky bacon. This mainly because it was sitting in the fridge but it does give a delicious flavour to the batter. Also I think a gravy of some sort is essential, either leftovers from Sunday's joint or a rich onion and red wine mixture such as the one following.

1 large egg
75ml/3fl oz milk
1 generous teaspoon made English mustard
50g/2oz plain flour (strong plain if you have it)
4 fat and meaty beef sausages
2 slices smoked streaky bacon, cut into small dice
about 2 tablespoons white vegetable fat

Preheat the oven to 220C/425F/gas mark 7. Whisk together the egg, milk and mustard with about 75ml/3fl oz of cold water. Put the flour into a bowl, make a dip in the middle and gradually whisk in the liquid. The batter should have the consistency of single cream. Leave the batter to sit at room temperature for 10–15 minutes while you brown the sausages. Snip the skin of each sausage and remove it. In a non-stick frying pan cook the bacon over a gentle heat until the fat runs, about 2–3 minutes. If the bacon was too lean and there is no fat then add a drizzle of oil to the pan. Now add the sausages and fry them over a slow heat until they are golden brown. This will take anything up to 10 minutes.

Transfer the sausage and bacon mixture to a shallow roasting tin with plenty of space for the batter to rise up and crisp. Add the vegetable fat and put the tin in the hot oven for about 5 minutes or until the fat is smoking hot and hazy. Pour the batter in and around the sausages (it should sizzle when it hits the fat) and return the tin to the oven straight away. Leave to cook for 20 minutes or until the batter has puffed up and is crisp and golden brown. Serve immediately with an Onion and Red Wine Gravy, see page 112.

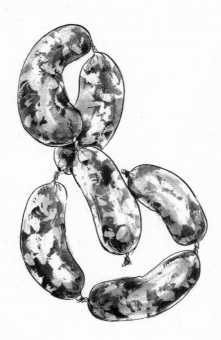

Onion and Red Wine Gravy
Serves 2

butter
1 large onion, finely chopped
about 1 teaspoon plain flour
½ teaspoon tomato purée (tomato ketchup is also fine if
    that's all you have)
½ teaspoon mustard, English, French or wholegrain
half a glass of red wine
about 150ml/5fl oz stock or water

Melt a good knob of butter in the frying pan and add the onion.
Cook it over a very low heat until it is a rich golden brown and
very soft. Increase the heat under the pan a little and continue
cooking the onion until it turns a dark caramel colour (be
careful not to burn the onion, as this will make the gravy bitter).

Sprinkle over the flour and stir it in over the heat until it
turns golden brown too. Add the tomato purée and mustard
followed by the wine and stock then bring everything to the
boil. Reduce the heat again and leave the gravy simmering
gently until required.

Sausages in Red Onion Marmalade
Serves 2

Happily there is something of a renaissance for sausages, with butchers offering many of their own recipes and supermarkets stocking an increasing number of premium brands. A garlicky Toulouse sausage works well here with the sweet sour flavour of the onions.

large knob of butter
225g/8 oz good quality sausages
2 large red onions, thinly sliced
small handful of chopped fresh thyme, or large pinch dried
1 glass red wine
50ml/2fl oz red wine vinegar
2 teaspoons granulated sugar
salt and freshly ground black pepper

Preheat the oven to 200C/400F/gas mark 6. Melt half the butter in a roasting tin and fry the sausages gently until just lightly browned. Add the remaining butter and all the onions and fry over a gentle heat for a good 10 minutes until they begin to soften. It will look as though you have too much onion for the tin but they do cook down.

Stir in all the remaining ingredients and bring to the boil. Lift the sausages to sit on top of the onions so that they continue to brown when cooking then place the roasting tin, uncovered, in the oven. Cook for about 45 minutes stirring occasionally. The onions should be soft, golden and glazed with the buttery pan juices.

You can cook ... the Red Onion Marmalade as above but without the sausages. Replace the sugar with a tablespoon of Crème de Cassis and serve with roast pork, duck or game.

Oven-baked Sausage and Bean Pot
Serves 2

A sausage hotpot makes a great autumn supper. Double up the quantities and cook it on bonfire night. It is one of those ideal dishes that is even better when made the day before. It can be reheated and sitting in the oven ready to serve when everyone comes in from the cold night air.

450g/1lb Toulouse sausages
sunflower or corn oil, if necessary
2 red onions, finely chopped
200ml/7fl oz light stock
350g pot chilled Arrabiatta or Napoletana pasta sauce
150ml/5fl oz Guinness
2 tablespoons light soft brown sugar
salt and freshly ground black pepper
400g can mixed cooked beans
1 small handful flat leaf parsley, chopped

Preheat the oven to 200C/400F/gas mark 6. Snip the sausage skins to let the fat run then brown them in a large, flameproof casserole or roasting tin over a moderate heat for 5 minutes. If there's very little fat from the sausages and they begin to stick add 1–2 tablespoons of oil.

Add the onions to the pan and fry until soft and golden brown, about 10 minutes. At this stage it will look as though you have too many onions but they do reduce down on cooking. There should be enough fat from the sausages to brown the onions but if not then add 1–2 tablespoons of oil.

Pour in the stock, Arrabiatta sauce, Guinness and brown sugar, and season. Bring to the boil and leave the mixture to bubble for 2 minutes while you drain the beans and rinse them in cold water. Stir the beans into the casserole and then put it in the oven for about 35–40 minutes until everything is bubbling and lightly browned on top. The liquid should have reduced down to barely cover the beans. The cooking time will depend on the size of casserole you use. If the liquid has not reduced down enough then pop it on the hob and bubble for 2–3 minutes to evaporate off a little more of the liquid. Stir well, then add in the parsley before serving.

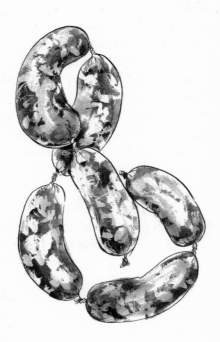

Venison Sausages with
Lentils and Red Wine
Serves 2

On a cold winter's night few suppers will warm you like this one – a rich pot of venison sausages and earthy lentils simmered with garlic and wine. Don't use anything but really tasty, meaty sausages, the ones that crumble when you cut them open. Try your local butcher first as most now sell excellent venison sausages or look at the supermarket's premium ranges, but keep to the simpler flavours.

You could use tinned lentils but it's really no faster. Green lentils cook in under 30 minutes so it's just as easy to do them while the sausages are simmering and then their texture is firmer and far better.

It's a simple recipe to double up if you're looking for a good supper dish for friends. Just multiply everything by two except the wine. Keep it at one glass but add about 150ml/5fl oz stock.

100g/4oz green lentils
olive oil
4–6 plump venison sausages, depending on your appetite
1 large red onion, peeled and cut into thin wedges from root
    to tip
2 garlic cloves, sliced
2 medium red peppers, halved, de-seeded and roughly
    chopped
1 large glass red wine
1 teaspoon redcurrant jelly
1 teaspoon English mustard
salt and freshly ground black pepper

Start cooking the lentils first. Put them in a saucepan and add enough boiling water to cover them by about 2.5cm/1 inch.

Bring back to the boil then simmer the lentils for about 25 minutes. Try one, it should be tender but still have a good 'bite' left.

While the lentils are cooking, heat 1 tablespoon of oil in a deep pan and brown the sausages all over till golden. Do this quite slowly over a medium heat then lift them out with a slotted spoon.

Add the onion, garlic and pepper to the pan with another tablespoon of oil if it looks dry and fry everything together until soft and beginning to brown at the edges. This will take a good 10 minutes or longer but be patient. The better the colour at this stage the better the 'sauce' will taste.

Drain the lentils and stir into the pan with the wine, redcurrant jelly and mustard, scraping up all the browned crusty bits from the bottom of the pan. Taste and season the liquid then pop the sausages on top and leave everything to simmer gently for about 10–15 minutes until the liquid has evaporated a little to form a sauce around the lentils and the sausages are tender.

I like a good winter green with this, steamed curly kale or Savoy cabbage would be favourites, plus some warm, nutty bread.

CHAPTER 4

Pasta and Risotto

Spaghetti with Crispy Garlic Crumbs
Serves 2

A cheap and cheerful supper that's very easily put together.
Add in anything else you have on hand – some chopped cooked
chicken, flakes of tuna or fresh crab, a handful of olives, capers
and anchovies perhaps, a pinch of dried chillies . . .

olive oil
2 fat garlic cloves, crushed
1½ slices fresh white bread made into rough breadcrumbs
knob of butter
salt and freshly ground black pepper
a small handful of chopped fresh chives and parsley
175g/6oz dried spaghetti or linguine pasta

Heat a drizzle of oil in a large frying pan and add the garlic and
breadcrumbs. Stir the crumbs over a medium heat for 4–5
minutes or until they turn a deep golden brown and crisp. Add
a touch more oil if necessary.

Add the butter, seasoning and herbs to the pan and set aside.
Cook the pasta in boiling, salted water until it is just tender then
drain well; toss with the crispy crumbs and serve.

Pappardelle with Sausage, Rosemary and Red Wine
Serves 2

I can't remember a week without pasta. It may be a soothing bowl of shells with a hot creamy sauce of melting Gorgonzola, a meaty Bolognese, rich and satisfying with plenty of salty Parmesan or simply a 10 minute supper of hot noodles tossed with my local deli's pesto sauce. There is always at least one night in the week when it just has to be pasta. Pappardelle – the broad noodle – is one of my favourites and is terrific with this sausage, red wine and tomato sauce. It's ready to eat in less than 30 minutes, tastes just as good the next day if you need to prepare ahead and freezes well too.

The better the sausage, the better the sauce. You need good, tasty, coarse-textured butcher's sausages for this, definitely not the pale pink and bland variety.

The addition of rosemary to this recipe is a recent one. It's really the only herb that survives in any quantity over the winter in my garden so I like to use it as often as I can, and I have found that its strong aromatic flavour works well.

olive oil
1 large Spanish onion, finely chopped
few sprigs fresh rosemary
1 small aubergine
4–6 plump, coarse sausages
a large glass gutsy red wine
300ml/½ pint passata (sieved tomatoes)
4 tablespoons chopped sun-dried tomatoes or a sun-dried
    tomato sauce
dried pappardelle noodles

Use a deep frying pan or shallow saucepan to cook the sauce as some of the liquid needs to evaporate away as it simmers. Add just enough olive oil to cover the bottom of the pan and cook the onions with the rosemary over a gentle heat for 10 minutes or so until they're completely soft and golden brown. You can't hurry this along; under-cooked onions are ghastly — bitter and indigestible. Stir in the aubergine and drizzle over a little more oil. Cook over a moderate heat until the aubergine is soft and beginning to brown at the edges. It will look a lot in the pan at first but the aubergine quickly cooks down.

While that's cooking skin the sausages. Tip the aubergine mixture onto a plate and crumble the sausages into the hot pan. You shouldn't need any extra oil at this stage. Stir the nuggets of meat over a high heat until they are well browned and crusty all over. Pour in the wine, it will bubble immediately, and leave to reduce by about half. Return the aubergine mixture with the passata and sun-dried tomatoes. Bubble gently for another 10 minutes or so then taste the sauce. It may need a pinch of sugar if the tomato is a little acidic.

If you're cooking the sauce to eat straight away . . . put a pan of water on to boil for the pasta when the aubergine is cooking. Pasta needs plenty of water and space to move around if you don't want a sticky mass so use a large saucepan. It's difficult for me to give pasta quantities, as I love to have much more sauce than pasta. For this recipe I will usually cook about 175g/6oz dried pappardelle noodles for two but you know your own taste and appetite and it is your supper after all. Don't forget to salt the water well, it does make a difference. Start cooking the pasta when the sauce is finally simmering. About 7–8 minutes should give soft noodles with just a bit of bite left. Drain the pasta; toss it with the sauce and a spoonful of grated Parmesan cheese. Hand round more of the cheese at the table.

Risotto with Two Cheeses
Serves 2

Next to pasta, risotto is one of the simplest and most satisfying suppers and just as variable. It's no trouble to cook as long as you remember three things:

• Always use a risotto rice. The grains are short, round and starchy and simply nothing else will give the risotto its characteristic velvety texture. Most good supermarkets now stock it either as 'risotto' or 'arborio' rice. Italian delicatessens will have arborio plus two or three others. My local deli also sells a 'quick cook' risotto rice that is sold loose but I've never had great success with it.

• The stock must always be added hot to the pan so have it gently bubbling beside you as you cook.

• Keep the risotto gently simmering and after about 15 minutes of cooking try the rice grains every minute or so. The risotto is ready when the rice is tender but with an easy bite left in it.

about 75g/3oz butter
1 medium onion, finely chopped
1 large garlic clove, peeled and sliced
225g/8oz risotto rice
about 750–900ml/1¼–1½ pints hot stock, chicken or
    vegetable
50g/2oz grated Parmesan cheese
salt and freshly ground black pepper
125g/4oz Mozzarella, Fontina or Taleggio cheese, diced

Melt about two-thirds of the butter in a shallow, heavy-based pan and add the onion and garlic. Cook over a moderate heat, stirring occasionally, until the onion is soft and beginning to turn golden. Don't try to hurry this, let the onion cook for a good 10 minutes to soften. Add the rice and stir it through the onion to coat the grains in butter. Ladle in about a third of the hot stock and lower the heat until the stock is just gently bubbling. Leave the risotto to simmer, stirring the rice from time to time, until the rice has soaked up almost all the stock. Add half the remaining stock and leave again, gently bubbling, until there's very little liquid left. The rice grains should be quite plump by now. Add the remaining stock a little at a time, stirring and tasting the rice until the grains are tender but still have a bit of bite left and the risotto looks creamy. All this sounds time consuming but the risotto should be ready in about 20 minutes.

Add the rest of the butter and the Parmesan cheese and stir until they have completely melted through the risotto. Taste it and season then stir in the diced cheese and serve immediately. The lumps will just be beginning to melt when you start to eat.

Two good variations on the above . . .

• Before you begin the risotto, put about 350g/12oz uncooked prawns (the grey ones) into the dry pan with 3–4 tablespoons of water. Stir them over a moderate heat for about 5–7 minutes or until they've lost their transparency and turned a soft pink. Remove the prawns from the pan and set them beside you while you make the risotto. While the rice is simmering and when the prawns are cool enough to handle, peel them. Stir the prawns into the risotto at the end with the butter and Parmesan.

• Fry 120g/4oz diced pancetta or bacon and 50g/2oz sliced flat mushrooms with the onion. Continue making the risotto as in the recipe above but don't add any cheese. Serve the risotto with softly poached eggs on top.

Gnocchi with Buttered Leeks and Gruyère
Serves 2

If you have never tried gnocchi let me tempt you by saying that these little dumplings are just as versatile as pasta and even quicker to cook. They can form the beginnings of any number of simple suppers. You'll find gnocchi beside the 'fresh' pasta in the chiller cabinet of most major supermarkets now and of course in good delis.

This particular gnocchi recipe is a heavenly mixture of buttery leeks, pesto and toasted cheese. It takes about 30 minutes to prepare and cook and is the type of supper to put on the table with a bowl of salad and some hot crusty bread.

If you don't want to fiddle about making white sauce then try one of the Tetra Paks of ready-made béchamel sauce sold in Italian delis. Don't turn your nose up! When mixed with strong flavours, as here, it's absolutely fine.

salt and freshly ground black pepper
500g/1lb gnocchi di patate (potato gnocchi)
50g/2oz butter
1 medium leek, chopped and rinsed
1 plump glove garlic, peeled and sliced
1 generous teaspoon pesto
25g/1oz flour
450ml/¾ pint milk
175g/6oz Gruyère cheese, coarsely grated
3 tablespoons mascarpone cheese

Bring a large, deep pan of water to the boil, salt it generously and drop in the gnocchi. When it comes back to the boil, turn down the heat a little and bubble the gnocchi for about 2–3 minutes, stirring all the time. Drain them well then put into a shallow, ovenproof dish.

Put the pan back on the heat (no need to rinse it) and melt half the butter. Add the leek and garlic and cook over a moderate heat, stirring occasionally, until the leek is soft and beginning to colour. Add the pesto, then tip the contents of the pan onto the gnocchi and stir through roughly.

Put the pan back on the heat (no need to rinse it) and melt the remaining butter. Stir in the flour to form a paste and cook for a couple of minutes until it turns a deep straw colour. Slowly pour in the milk, stirring or whisking over a moderate heat until the sauce comes up to the boil. Simmer gently for 4–5 minutes until lightly thickened and smooth. (If using ready-made béchamel sauce thin it down a little with milk to give a thin pouring sauce and simmer until piping hot before adding the cheese etc.)

Remove the sauce from the heat and stir in about two thirds of the grated cheese and all the mascarpone. Season the sauce, remembering that both the cheese and the pesto are quite salty. Pour the sauce over the gnocchi and sprinkle over the remaining cheese.

Put under a hot grill for 2–3 minutes until golden brown and well toasted. Eat immediately.

Try . . .

• A handful of chopped pancetta or streaky bacon fried with the leek before stirring it through the pasta.

• Grilled and chopped red peppers when leeks are no longer around.

• Different cheeses. Use up any bits of strong cheese you may have that have passed their best.

Pasta with Pesto and Fresh Peas
Serves 2

Summer suppers don't come any better (or simpler) than a bowl of hot pasta with a dollop of homemade pesto and some fresh, shelled peas or beans.

I can still remember tasting my first fresh pea as a child. Standing dwarfed by the towering canes, I thought that nothing had ever tasted quite like it. I still wallow in nostalgia whenever I shell peas from the pod and invariably eat as many as I put in the pot. If podding peas doesn't hold the same appeal for you then opt for one of the packs of fresh, shelled peas that most of the supermarkets now stock.

However, there really is no excuse for not making your own pesto in summer when basil is so plentiful and it's ready in less time than it takes to cook the pasta. No shop-bought pesto can shake a stick at one you'll make at home. The best pesto is undoubtedly made in a pestle and mortar but it does take more time.

I've added some diced mozzarella cheese because I love the way it melts through the pesto but the supper is just as good without.

175g/6oz dried pasta
salt
a large handful of fresh basil leaves (about 50g/2oz or 4 of
    the small, supermarket packs)
small handful pine nuts, lightly toasted if time allows
2–3 garlic cloves
6–8 tablespoons extra virgin olive oil
5 tablespoons finely grated Parmesan cheese
1 mozzarella cheese, cut into small cubes
225g/8oz fresh shelled peas or broad beans

Drop the pasta into a large pan of boiling, salted water and cook until just tender, about 7–10 minutes depending on the shape.

While the pasta is cooking tear the basil leaves into a food processor with the pine nuts, garlic, pinch of salt and 6 tablespoons olive oil. Whiz together until you have a thick and speckled, bright green paste, pushing the mixture down from time to time with a spatula. Take care not to over process; the pesto should look quite rough. Transfer to a bowl and stir in the Parmesan cheese and mozzarella.

Add the peas to the boiling pasta for the last 3–4 minutes of cooking time. When both are tender reserve 3–4 tablespoons of the cooking water then drain the pasta into a colander. Return the pasta and peas to the pot. Add the reserved water to the pesto and a little extra olive oil to give the sauce a soft creamy consistency. Gently stir in enough pesto to coat the hot pasta and serve immediately.

Try . . .

• Any leftover pesto can be kept in a jar in the fridge for about a week. Flood a little extra olive oil on top then cover with a lid or clingfilm.

• The basil, pinenut and olive oil mixture can be frozen without the addition of the cheeses.

• Any other buttery, melting cheese can be stirred through the pesto; try Fontina or Taleggio. Or grill rounds of chèvre till golden and bubbling and pop on top of the hot pasta just before serving.

Three Cheese Macaroni
Serves 2

At its most basic macaroni cheese makes a blissfully simple supper – hot, soft and melting underneath and toasted on top. A little more imagination and it can be turned, quite effortlessly, into something sublime. In this recipe I've replaced the traditional Cheddar with three Italian cheeses: Fontina which is mild and buttery, mozzarella for its creamy texture and Parmesan for its distinctive salty 'bite'. The result is a rich, smooth gratin that is ready to eat in around 30 minutes.

    salt and freshly ground black pepper
    175g/6oz dried macaroni or any other small pasta shape
    40g/1½oz butter
    1 bay leaf
    25g/1oz flour
    600ml/1pint milk
    175g/6oz Fontina cheese, roughly chopped
    a generous teaspoon of Dijon mustard
    large pinch ground nutmeg
    75g/3oz mozzarella cheese, roughly chopped
    40g/1½oz freshly grated Parmesan cheese
    small palmful of fresh white breadcrumbs

Bring a deep saucepan of water to the boil, add a good pinch of salt and drop in the macaroni. Let the water return to the boil then reduce the heat a little and bubble the pasta until it is just tender, about 7–10 minutes. Drain the pasta well and set it aside while you make the sauce.

Melt the butter in the same saucepan then stir in the bay leaf and flour. Cook for a minute or two until the paste turns a deep, creamy colour. Pour in the milk then stir or whisk vigorously over a medium heat until you have a smooth sauce. Simmer the sauce very gently for about 10 minutes, stirring from time to time.

Take the sauce off the heat and remove the bay leaf. Stir in the Fontina, mustard and nutmeg then taste and season carefully with salt (remember that two of the cheeses themselves are quite salty) and plenty of ground black pepper.

Mix the remaining mozzarella and about half the Parmesan into the sauce with all the macaroni. Put the pan back on the heat and stir for 1–2 minutes just until the pasta is piping hot again then tip into a shallow, heatproof dish.

Sprinkle the top with the remaining Parmesan cheese and the breadcrumbs and pop under a hot grill for 2–3 minutes until golden brown and crispy then serve immediately.

Pasta with Chicken Liver, Sausage and Chilli Sauce
Serves 2

I am a big fan of chicken livers. Pan-fried with little lardons of bacon until the outside is golden, crusty and caramelized and the inside just pink and velvety, these plump little nuggets can make a sensational supper served on a bed of soft salad leaves. Perfect too if you're in a hurry for the quicker they're cooked the more succulent they'll be. Although it's still quite difficult to buy them fresh (unless you're blessed with a good butcher) most supermarkets sell them frozen. This is a gutsy sauce for pasta with plenty of spicy sausage and tomato. If chicken livers really don't appeal then you can top up with extra sausage.

> 225g/8oz chicken livers
> 125g/4oz coarse, spicy pork or lamb sausages
> olive oil
> a good knob of butter
> 1 small onion, finely chopped
> a little chopped red chilli, no more than a large pinch unless
>   you want the sauce fiery
> small glass of dry white wine
> 150ml/5fl oz passata with basil
> 1 generous tablespoon sun-dried tomato paste
> freshly grated Parmesan cheese or crumbled Feta cheese

Wash the chicken livers then pat them dry on kitchen paper. They're usually well trimmed but snip off any sinews and cut away any green patches that you may find. Split the sausages open, take off the skin and crumble the meat.

Heat a little oil in a deep frying pan and add the butter. When it starts to sizzle drop in the chicken livers and cook over a fierce heat for about a minute on each side until they are brown on the outside but still feel soft to touch. Remove them from the pan and set on one side. Roughly crumble the sausage meat into the pan and fry it, stirring all the time, until it too is golden brown and cooked through. Remove and set aside with the livers.

Now add the onion and chilli and cook over a lower heat until the onion is golden and quite soft (there should be enough fat left in the pan). This will take a good 10 minutes.

Pour in the wine, scraping up any bits from the bottom of the pan as it bubbles, then add the passata and sun-dried tomato paste. Bring slowly to a gentle simmer and leave to cook for one to two minutes.

Return the chicken livers and sausage to the pan with any juices that have run out and stir briefly over the heat for just two minutes then take it off. Serve the sauce on piping hot pasta with plenty of grated Parmesan or crumbled Feta cheese.

Ideally . . . this pasta sauce should be made and served straight away, as over-cooked chicken livers are just disastrous. If you're using dried pasta put a large pan of water on to boil before you begin the sauce. The water should be boiling by the time the onion has softened so add the pasta then with a couple of good pinches of salt and hopefully everything should be ready together.

Meatballs with Olive and Pesto Pasta
Serves 2

Really good meatballs made with minced meat and plenty of flavourings – garlic, herbs and spices – are delicious with pasta. An easy way to make 'home-made' meatballs is to take one of the rough, garlicky sausages now in butchers and supermarkets and quickly convert them.

> 225g/8oz good-quality coarse lamb or beef sausages
> olive oil
> 1 red onion, sliced
> 125g/4oz *fresh* egg spaghetti or pappardelle noodles
> a handful black olives
> small handful chopped fresh parsley or chives (or both)
> 2 tablespoons pesto sauce (see page 128 for home-made)

Slit the sausages from top to bottom with a sharp knife then peel off the skin. Break each sausage in half and roll each piece into a ball then flatten slightly. Heat a drizzle of oil in a large, non-stick saucepan and fry the meatballs for 5 minutes or until golden brown all over. Lift out and set aside on a plate.

Add the onion to the pan and fry until it is very soft and golden. (Remember to allow a good 8–10 minutes for this or the onion will still be bitter and indigestible in the finished sauce.) Add the onions to the meatballs.

Put the pasta in the saucepan (there's no need to wash it out as the oil from the frying will help to keep the pasta separate) and pour over boiling water to cover. Bring to the boil and cook until just tender. Drain the pasta and return it to the pan. Stir the olives, herbs and pesto into the pasta, then return the meatballs and onions and any juices which have collected on the plate.

Shake gently over the heat rather than stir to warm

everything through without breaking up the meatballs. Serve each portion of pasta on piping hot plates and eat at once.

A squeeze of lemon juice . . . over the top will sharpen the flavours if the pesto sauce is very salty.

Look out for . . . Niçoise olives. They're much smaller than the more common varieties but have a wonderful flavour. When using olives such as these, that always have the stone in, it's a good idea to put them in a polythene bag and hit them lightly with a rolling pin! This gently crushes the olives, releasing their natural juices and making the stones easier to release.

The only golden rule . . . for serving pasta is to allow plenty of sauce. It can be a little under-cooked or even over-cooked and almost anything can be tossed in but always have plenty of sauce. Pesto is one of the classics and is hard to beat, but this easy cream sauce is just as good. Warm together a 284ml/10fl oz carton single cream with 125g/4oz Gorgonzola and a sprig of fresh rosemary. Toss through enough hot pasta for four before serving.

Garlic and Parmesan Risotto
Serves 2

a knob of butter
1 large onion, finely chopped
1 sprig fresh rosemary if you have it
3 garlic cloves
125g/4oz risotto rice
350ml/12fl oz hot, light stock with a splash of white wine
    added
25g/1oz freshly grated Parmesan cheese
small handful chopped fresh flatleaf parsley

Melt half the butter in a large, heavy-based saucepan and stir in the onion and rosemary if using. Cook for 8–10 minutes until very soft but not too coloured then stir in the crushed garlic and rice. Stir thoroughly over the heat for 1–2 minutes to coat the rice lightly in the butter.

Pour in a ladleful of the hot stock and let it simmer gently, stirring now and again until the rice has absorbed most of it. Keep adding the stock in this way until all the stock has been used and the rice tender but still has a bite to it. The risotto should look creamy and soft. Stir in the remaining butter, Parmesan cheese and parsley.

Enjoy this as a simple supper on its own or try adding one of the following ...

• Stir 125g/4oz diced Mozzarella cheese into the risotto just before serving and it will just be beginning to melt when you start to eat.

• With the last ladleful of stock add 225g/8oz flaked salmon fillet. Simmer with the risotto for a minute until cooked then stir in 125g/4oz cooked, peeled prawns and a large spoonful of sun-dried tomato paste. Heat through for a further minute before serving. Chopped basil rather than rosemary and parsley would be good too.

• Fry 125g/4oz chopped smoked back bacon and 50g/2oz sliced mushrooms with the rice. Continue as above but omit the Parmesan cheese and serve with softly boiled or poached eggs. Add some diced and fried black pudding too for a great Sunday brunch!

Monday Night Risotto
Serves 2

Some of the most enjoyable suppers I've had have been made from leftovers found lurking in the fridge on a Monday evening. My favourite is roast chicken stripped from the bones plus the rich, brown jelly saved from the roasting tin stirred into risotto. And this one is especially simple; it needs no attention as it simmers in the oven. It can also be made without the leftovers and served as a partner to pan-fried escalopes of pork or grilled chicken.

> a large knob of butter
> 1 small onion, chopped
> 125g/4oz brown cap, chestnut or shitake mushrooms, sliced
> 75g/3oz risotto (arborio) rice
> 300ml/½ pint stock (could be leftover gravy and stock
>   mixed)
> small glass of dry sherry
> about 125g/4oz leftover roast cut into strips, chicken, turkey
>   or ham
> 25g/1oz freshly grated Parmesan cheese
> salt and freshly ground black pepper
> lemon wedges for squeezing

Melt the butter in a small ovenproof casserole and fry the onion and mushrooms together until the onion is soft and a good golden brown. Stir in the rice making sure all the grains are coated in the buttery mixture, then add the stock and sherry. Bring to the boil and cook, uncovered, at 180C/350F/gas mark 4 for 15–20 minutes or until the rice has completely absorbed the liquid. Stir in the strips of meat with about half of the cheese. Taste for seasoning and sprinkle the remaining cheese on top before serving. I like to squeeze a bit of lemon juice on top too.

Chilli Noodles and Prawns
Serves 2

175g/6oz dried linguine pasta
salt and freshly ground black pepper
a good drizzle of olive oil
1 shallot or small red onion, finely chopped
1 garlic clove, thinly sliced
½ small red chilli, de-seeded and chopped or a pinch of
    dried chilli flakes
small glass of dry white wine
200g can chopped tomatoes
125g/4oz cooked, peeled prawns or flaked, fresh white crab
    meat
small handful flatleaf parsley, roughly chopped

Cook the pasta in a large pot of boiling, salted water until just tender. While the pasta is cooking heat a drizzle of oil in a frying pan and add the onion, garlic and chilli. Cook over a medium heat until the onion is soft and golden then add the wine. Let it bubble for 2–3 minutes then stir in the tomatoes. Keep stirring over the heat for a further 2–3 minutes then add the prawns and parsley. Take the pan off the heat now. Drain the pasta well and stir in the prawn sauce. Serve as fast as you can!

Gnocchi Puttanesca
Serves 2

Puttanesca is a spicy sauce for pasta that's made with onions, tomatoes, capers, anchovies, olives and herbs. You will be able to find it ready-made in most supermarkets but it's so easy to do at home and far superior when the flavours are fresh. Don't just keep it for gnocchi or pasta: it's a winner with grilled chicken, pan-fried fish, and sausages too.

a drizzle of olive oil
1 small onion, finely chopped
1 fat garlic clove, crushed
25g anchovy fillets in oil, chopped
½ small red chilli, de-seeded and chopped
4 ripe plum tomatoes, coarsely chopped
about 2 teaspoons capers, chopped
salt and freshly ground black pepper
400g gnocchi con patate or 175g/6oz dried pasta
small handful pitted, black olives
a small handful chopped fresh basil or parsley
Parmesan cheese

Heat about 2 tablespoons of oil in a pan and add the onion, garlic, anchovies and chilli. Cook, stirring, for about 10 minutes or until the onions are soft and golden. Add the tomatoes and capers and cook over a gentle heat for a further 10 minutes or until the tomatoes are softened and pulpy. Taste and add seasoning. If you're making this sauce out of the tomato season then you may want to add in the tiniest pinch of sugar as the tomatoes may be a little acidic.

Meanwhile, cook the gnocchi in a large pan of boiling, salted water for 2–3 minutes, or until they pop up to the surface. Drain them well and return to the pan with the tomato sauce, olives and basil or parsley. Toss well and serve immediately with plenty of freshly grated Parmesan cheese.

Spaghetti with Toasted Walnuts
and Smoky Bacon Sauce
Serves 2

This is simply a marriage made in heaven. Toasted creamy goat's cheese, crispy bacon and walnuts. Divine! I cannot think of any other cheese that would work as well toasted so if you really don't like goat's then have the pasta with some grated Parmesan instead.

175g/6oz dried spaghetti
salt and freshly ground black pepper
olive oil
150g/5oz rindless smoked back bacon, roughly chopped
1 garlic clove, crushed
a small handful of walnut pieces, chopped
225g/8oz ripe plum tomatoes, chopped
a small handful chopped fresh flatleaf parsley
squeeze of lemon juice
2 thick rounds of fresh goat's cheese

Cook the pasta in boiling, salted water until just tender. While the pasta is cooking, heat a drizzle of oil in a large, shallow pan and fry the bacon, garlic and walnuts together until golden brown and the bacon is beginning to crisp around the edges. Stir in the tomatoes and parsley and stir over the heat for a further minute.

Drain the pasta and toss with the walnut and bacon sauce. Spoon into hot, heatproof plates or bowls and top each one with a round of goat's cheese. Pop under a hot grill for 2–3 minutes or until the cheese turns golden and begins to bubble. Enjoy!

Stir-fried Pork with Cappelletti and Mustard
Serves 2

Of course you don't have to use cappelletti pasta here, you can use any shape you want, but I like the little caps for they catch the sauce well. If you have any single or soured cream in the fridge, add a spoonful or two just at the end of cooking.

75g/3oz dried pasta such as cappelletti or orecchiette
salt and freshly ground black pepper
olive oil
1 garlic clove, crushed
225g/8oz pork fillet, thinly sliced
a large knob of butter
125g/4oz chestnut mushrooms, sliced
1 generous tablespoon coarse grain mustard
a small handful chopped fresh chives or spring onions

Cook the pasta in boiling, salted water until just tender. While the pasta is cooking, heat a drizzle of oil with the garlic in a large, shallow pan. Fry the pork over a high heat until it is a good golden brown colour. Remove from the pan and set aside. Add the butter to the pan and fry the mushrooms until browned.

Drain the pasta, reserving 2 to 3 tablespoons of liquid. Stir the pasta and liquid into the pan with the pork, mustard and chives. Keep stirring for 1–2 minutes until everything is piping hot then serve.

Mushroom and Pancetta Linguine
Serves 2

olive oil
1 large onion, finely chopped
2 garlic cloves, crushed
large pinch chopped fresh red chilli or dried chilli flakes or a
    few drops of chilli sauce
50g/2oz pancetta or streaky bacon
225g/8oz chestnut mushrooms
1 generous glass red wine
400g can chopped tomatoes
1 tablespoon sun-dried tomato paste or red pesto
1 teaspoon sugar
175g/6oz dried linguine pasta

Heat a drizzle of oil in a large saucepan and fry the onion gently with the crushed garlic and chilli for at least 10 minutes or until very soft and golden brown. Add the bacon and mushrooms and continue to cook, stirring all the time, for a further 10 minutes until all the liquid has evaporated and the bacon is golden and the mushrooms are cooked through.

Add the red wine and bring to the boil. Bubble the wine for about 2 minutes before stirring in the tomatoes, paste and sugar. Taste for seasoning then simmer gently, uncovered, for 10–15 minutes.

While the sauce is simmering, cook the pasta in plenty of boiling, salted water. Drain the pasta well and stir it into the hot mushroom sauce.

Noodles with Hot Ham
and Parmesan Cream
Serves 2

I never tire of this recipe. This is one of my favourite suppers when fresh asparagus is in season and it's so quick. Both pasta and sauce take just ten minutes to cook.

225g/8oz fresh asparagus, cut into small finger lengths
salt and freshly ground black pepper
1 small leek or 2 or 3 spring onions, finely chopped
125g/4oz dried, broad pasta noodles
25g/1oz Parma ham or wafer thin cooked ham, roughly
    chopped
about 6–8 tablespoons single cream
25g/1oz freshly grated Parmesan cheese

Cook the asparagus in boiling, salted water for 7–10 minutes or until it is just tender. Add the leeks or spring onions to the pan for the last 30 seconds, then drain well.

While the vegetables are cooking drop the pasta into a pan of boiling, salted water and cook until tender, then drain. Toss together the pasta, vegetables, ham, cream and half the cheese. Serve straight away and sprinkle the extra cheese on top before serving.

Lamb and Rosemary Ragu
Serves 4

Thank goodness for pasta! It's the answer for supper so many times whether I need to cook something in 10 minutes, feed a hungry teenager or produce a miracle from the storecupboard! There are literally dozens of ready-made pasta sauces in the supermarkets now and I think I've tried most of them. For me, many of the jars are too thick and heavily seasoned with strong, dried herbs but I do like some of the tubs of chilled tomato sauces. They freeze well and can easily be jazzed up with a few clever additions.

The following sauce can be made using minced lamb or beef. It's enough for four people but it freezes well.

350g/12oz minced lamb
1 large onion, finely chopped
1 sprig fresh rosemary or large pinch dried
1 large glass red wine, about 200ml/7fl oz
350g tub chilled fresh Napoletana (or similar fresh tomato) sauce
salt and freshly ground black pepper

Brown the mince in a non-stick pan, stirring to break down any lumps. Take a good 5–7 minutes to do this, getting the mince a dark golden brown at this stage really adds to the flavour of the finished sauce. Remove the mince and set aside. Add the onion to the pan with the rosemary (there should be enough fat left from the mince without having to add any extra oil) and fry together until the onion is soft and golden, again about 10 minutes. Return the mince, keep the pan over a high heat and stir in the wine, which will bubble immediately. Scrape the bottom of the pan to loosen any crusty bits then leave the wine to bubble gently until half of it has evaporated, just a minute or two. Stir in the sauce then cover and simmer very gently for about 20 minutes. Check the seasoning before serving.

Stir . . . the Lamb and Rosemary Ragu into 350g/12oz dried spaghetti cooked in boiling, salted water for about 10 minutes. Grated Parmesan cheese is of course the traditional cheese to serve with pasta but I've found that Feta or goat's cheese also goes well with this. Either crumble the cheese or pare it with a vegetable peeler into wafer thin slices.

CHAPTER 5

Eggs, Bacon, Pastries, Potatoes etc!

Baked Eggs on Roasted Pepper 'Stew'

Serves 2

Another easy recipe that requires little preparation. Plum or vine tomatoes are definitely the best, as they tend to have the most flavour.

2 red peppers, roughly chopped
1 large red onion, roughly chopped
½ red chilli, de-seeded and chopped
3 garlic cloves
pinch sugar
4 plum or vine tomatoes, halved and de-seeded
salt and freshly ground black pepper
olive oil
2 tablespoons sun-dried tomato paste
4 small eggs
small handful chopped fresh flatleaf parsley, chives or thyme

Put the peppers, onion, chilli, garlic and sugar in a small roasting tin with half the tomatoes. Add plenty of seasoning and drizzle lightly with olive oil. Roast the vegetables at 220C/425F/gas mark 7 for about 20 minutes, stirring now and again. Push the remaining four tomato halves into the roasted vegetables and pop back in the oven for a further 10–15 minutes until soft and lightly charred.

Now crack an egg into each tomato half, season well and spoon over any pan juices. Return to the oven for 5–7 minutes or until the eggs are just set but still wobbly.

Soured Cream and
Caramelized Onion Tarts
Makes 6

If you have the time it's worth making a few of these pastries and freezing them raw. They make a good light supper or a tasty starter with some peppery salad leaves. Try the soured cream pastry even if, like me, you don't normally make your own pastry. You won't regret it. It emerges from the oven buttery and flaky like an old-fashioned rough puff.

150g/5oz chilled butter, diced
175g/6oz plain flour
6–7 level tablespoons soured cream
4 tablespoons olive oil
900g/2lb onions, peeled and sliced
small handful pinenuts
small handful raisins
125g/4oz Feta cheese, crumbled
25g/1oz each pitted black olives and sun-dried tomatoes,
    roughly chopped
small handful capers

Make sure the butter is very cold and put it in a food processor with the flour. Pulse until the butter is roughly chopped through the flour, then add the soured cream and pulse again for 2–3 seconds until it is just mixed. It will look very rough.

On a floured surface, cut the pastry into six and thinly roll out each into a 15cm/6 inch diameter round. Place on two baking sheets, then cover and chill for 30 minutes.

Preheat the oven to 200C/400F/gas mark 6. Heat the oil in a large frying pan. Add the onions and cook over a low heat for 10–15 minutes, stirring occasionally, until they're very well reduced down, soft and a deep golden brown.

Set the onions aside to cool, then stir in the pinenuts, raisins, cheese, olives, tomatoes and capers. Spoon the onion mixture into the centre of the pastries leaving about a 2.5cm/1 inch clear edge. Roughly fold up the pastry edges around the filling, then cook for about 30 minutes or until golden.

Spiced Aubergine and Sweet Potato Stew
Serves 4

I hate the phrase 'storecupboard supper' for it conjures up images of dry tuna bakes and tinned tomatoes on toast, but when life is hectic I often turn to this mildly spiced stew of aubergine and sweet potato to provide an almost instant meal. It's the most delightful combination, even though three of the ingredients are from cans. It's also easily adapted to use whatever else is on hand. The basic sauce of onion, spices, tomato and coconut milk can be cooked with pumpkin, spinach, leftover potatoes, lentils etc. I've also dropped cubes of fish or chicken breast fillets into the simmering sauce to cook for a 'meatier' version. Try it on Boxing Day with any leftover turkey.

Because the recipe relies on cans, it's difficult to cook for less than four but the cooked stew does freeze well so you could put half in the freezer for another evening.

Plain basmati rice is perfect with the stew or simply scoop it up with some warm naan bread.

olive oil
1 medium aubergine, cut into large chunks, a bit bigger than bite-sized
1 medium onion, chopped
a generous thumb-sized piece of fresh root ginger, peeled
1 tablespoon garam masala or a mild curry paste
400g can chickpeas
1 large sweet potato, peeled and cut into large chunks
400g can chopped tomatoes
400g can coconut milk
salt and freshly ground black pepper
a handful of fresh coriander (not essential)

Heat about 4 tablespoons oil in a saucepan and fry the aubergine until it is golden brown and beginning to soften. Lift it out on to a plate with a draining spoon then add another 1–2 tablespoons oil to the pan and fry the onion for at least 10 minutes until it is soft and golden. Coarsely grate the ginger into the onions, stir over the heat for a couple of minutes then add the garam masala. Reduce the heat a little and cook the spices with the onions and ginger for 1–2 minutes.

Drain and rinse the chickpeas, then add to the pan with the sweet potato, tomatoes and coconut milk. Bring to the boil then turn down to a simmer. Cook everything gently together until the sweet potato is just tender, about 10–12 minutes. Taste the stew and add some seasoning.

If you have some coriander, roughly chop it and stir in just before eating.

A word of warning . . . if you've never bought sweet potatoes – there are often two varieties to choose from. The one to buy for its nutty flavour has an orange flesh; the other is white and tends to be sweet and starchy. Most supermarkets only stock the former but some markets and Asian greengrocers have both so take care.

Aubergine, Pepper and Basil Parmigiana
Serves 2

This supper isn't as much trouble to make as it may at first appear. It takes just 10–15 minutes to slice and grill the aubergines and peppers, then they will reward you with their intense, smoky flavour and voluptuous texture. Teamed with some peppery basil leaves, tomato sauce and buttery cheese they can turn quite effortlessly into a simple supper. The idea works well for larger quantities too, and I've often made this as an accompaniment to barbecued food.

I'm always very happy to cheat and use a good quality, ready-made tomato sauce but I've also included a recipe for a homemade one that freezes well. I tend to use canned plum tomatoes for this as most of our homegrown tomatoes, even at the height of summer, aren't that good and often lack the intense flavour needed for the sauce.

Finally, if you're buying basil in the supermarkets the little flat packs of larger leaves tend to have more flavour than the leaves of the young plants in pots.

2 large red peppers
1 large aubergine
2–3 fat garlic cloves, sliced
olive oil
½ quantity Simple Tomato Sauce (see page 158) *or*
350g jar good quality tomato sauce such as Loyd Grossman's
    Tomato & Basil or Primavera or 200ml chilled
    Napoletana sauce
small handful basil leaves, roughly chopped
125g/4oz Fontina cheese or a buttery Cheddar, coarsely
    grated
25g/1oz freshly grated Parmesan cheese
black pepper

Quarter the peppers and remove all the seeds and core. Cut the aubergine lengthways into thin slices. Put the pepper, aubergine and garlic on a grill rack, season lightly with salt and pepper then brush generously with oil. Place under the grill for about 5–6 minutes until the peppers are blackened and soft, then remove them to a bowl and leave to cool a little. Put the aubergine back under the grill for an extra 2–3 minutes until golden brown and crisp in places. (There should be some juices in the grill pan. Tip these into the tomato sauce.)

When the grilled pepper is cool enough to handle, peel off the skins. It doesn't matter if the odd bit of charred skin remains.

Preheat the oven to 200C/400F/gas mark 6. Spoon a little of the tomato sauce over the bottom of an oiled, ovenproof dish then cover it with a layer of aubergine and pepper. Sprinkle with a little of the basil and some of the coarsely grated cheese. Repeat the layers of sauce, aubergine etc until everything has been used and finish with a layer of cheese. Sprinkle with the Parmesan cheese and season with pepper. Bake for about 30 minutes or until golden brown. Pop under the grill for 1–2 minutes if necessary.

Serve with crusty garlic bread and a salad.

A Simple Tomato Sauce
Serves 4 with pasta

1 medium onion, finely chopped
2 garlic cloves, crushed
50g/2oz butter
900g/2lbs very ripe tomatoes *or* 2 x 400g cans plum
    tomatoes, roughly chopped
3 tablespoons sun-dried tomato paste or pesto
1 tablespoon chopped basil, marjoram or oregano
salt and freshly ground black pepper
large pinch sugar

Fry the onion and garlic in the butter until soft and golden. Add all the remaining ingredients then simmer, uncovered, over a low heat until the sauce is thick and pulpy. Taste the sauce and season with salt, pepper and a pinch of sugar if the tomatoes are very acidic.

Shortcut Shortcrust
Makes about 225g/8oz pastry

150g/5oz plain flour
50g/2oz butter
15g/½oz white vegetable fat
pinch salt

Put everything in a food processor and blend with the pulse
button until the mixture looks like rough breadcrumbs. Add a
generous tablespoon of chilled water and pulse again until the
dough just begins to come together. It may need a little more
water. Don't over process it or the pastry will be tough. Chill
the pastry while you cook the filling.

Green Tomato and Mayonnaise Tart
Serves 4

If, like me, you're often looking at pounds of green, unripened fruit on your tomato plants by the end of the summer this recipe will come as a welcome change to making chutney. It's a rough-crusted, throw-it-in-the-oven type of tart that takes no skill to do and is perfect served warm with salad for a late supper.

A crisp and buttery home-made crust will always win over a bought pastry but as it's something tasty to eat we're after and not a Michelin star, a ready-made shortcrust will be absolutely fine here – and it does save time and mess.

> 1 small red onion, finely chopped
> olive oil
> 225g/8oz green or firm tomatoes
> 1 garlic clove
> salt and ground black pepper
> 125g/4oz mayonnaise
> 125g/4oz mature Cheddar cheese or Gruyère, coarsely
>   grated
> small handful fresh basil, roughly chopped
> 225g/8oz shortcrust pastry (see page 159, Shortcut
>   Shortcrust)

Cook the onion in a drizzle of oil until soft and golden brown. This will take a good ten minutes in a frying pan over a moderate heat. Don't try to rush it, as the onion does need to be soft before adding the tomatoes. While the onion is cooking, cut the tomatoes into slices about as thick as a pound coin. Add to the softened onion with the crushed garlic and leave to cook, turning once or twice, for about 3–4 minutes. The tomatoes should just begin to soften around the edges. Season with a little salt (not too much as the cheese is quite salty) and a generous grinding of black pepper.

Beat together the mayonnaise, cheese and basil. Preheat the oven to 200C/400F/gas mark 6 and put in a baking sheet to heat up. Take the pastry from the fridge and cut in half. Roll each piece into a rough circle at least 15cm/6 inch wide. Roll the pastry rounds onto a floured rolling pin and unroll onto a sheet of foil.

Stir the mayonnaise into the tomatoes then spoon the mixture (it will look a mess) into the centre of each pastry round in a pile leaving about a 2.5cm/1 inch clear edge. Fold up and pinch the pastry edges very roughly over the filling just as far as they will go. Don't worry, they're not intended to meet in the middle.

Slide the pastries, still on the foil, onto the hot baking sheet. (This may appear strange and a bit of a fiddle but putting the pastry onto a hot baking sheet helps to cook the base and avoid a soggy bottom.) Dab a little milk or beaten egg over the pastry edges and bake the tarts in the hot oven for about 30 minutes or until golden brown and lightly set. Allow to cool for 10 minutes before eating.

Slow-cooked Onions with Melting Cheese
Serves 2

Many of the letters I receive each week are pleas for long lost recipes: sticky school puddings, old-fashioned biscuits and childhood teatime treats are all regular requests. Each one is wishing to savour again a much-loved taste from the past. One of my all-time childhood favourites, and luckily one which needs no recipe, is a supper my father used to make for myself and my brother on the rare occasions he had to cook tea for us. It was a dish my grandmother had made for him and is now one of my regulars when I want something deeply savoury and easy to serve with a salad. It is quite simply slow-cooked onions with melting cheese. I've adapted it slightly; my father would spoon it still sizzling onto hot, buttered toast and now I bake it on thin rounds of mustard-laced puff pastry or spoon it into hot, baked potatoes. It's the easiest supper in the world and to me one of the most delicious too.

    3 large Spanish onions, thinly sliced
    butter
    1 sheet ready-rolled puff pastry, about 200g
    2 tablespoons wholegrain mustard
    ground black pepper
    75–100g/3–4oz cheese such as mature Cheddar, Gruyère or
        Leerdammer, coarsely grated
    a little beaten egg or milk

Put the onions in a heavy frying pan with a good knob of butter and leave them to cook slowly over a moderate heat until they have turned a pale golden colour and are very soft and tender. Allow a good 30 minutes for this.

While the onions are cooking, unroll the puff pastry and roll it out even more – as thin as you dare. Using a tea plate as a guide, cut two large circles and put them on one large or two small baking sheets. Preheat the oven to 220C/425F/gas mark 7. Prick the pastry all over with a fork, spread with the mustard and return it to the fridge until ready to cook.

Increase the heat under the onions, season with plenty of pepper, and cook them for another 5–7 minutes, stirring all the time, until any remaining liquid in the pan has bubbled away and the onions are a deep golden brown and slightly charred here and there.

Stir the grated cheese into the sizzling onions and spoon onto the pastry rounds. Spread evenly over the pastry leaving a narrow, clear edge. Brush this edge with beaten egg or milk and bake the pastries for about 15 minutes or until golden brown and toasted on top.

Serve straight away with a fresh tomato salad, dressed with a sharp vinaigrette and sprinkled with some chopped fresh thyme.

When sun-ripened tomatoes are available . . . thinly slice 2 or 3 depending on size and put a circle of them in the centre of each round before baking.

Mushroom and Feta Omelette
Serves 2

This is not strictly an omelette as there are more 'extras' than egg. It's a mix of fried mushrooms, sun-dried tomatoes and garlic bound together with a little beaten egg then topped and grilled with salty Feta cheese. Depending on the size of your non-stick pans you can either make one large omelette and cut it into wedges or fry the mushrooms etc. as in step 1, then make 2 individual omelettes.

Remember that both Feta cheese and sun-dried tomatoes can be salty so no extra should be needed to season the omelette.

a large knob of butter
175g/6oz flat large mushrooms, thinly sliced
1 garlic clove, sliced
6–8 sun-dried or sun-blush tomatoes
3 eggs, beaten with 30ml/2 tablespoons water
125g/4oz Feta cheese, crumbled
freshly ground black pepper
chopped flat leaf parsley

Melt the butter in a non-stick pan and fry the mushrooms with the garlic until they are a deep golden brown and there's no liquid left in the pan. Add the tomatoes and stir over the heat for 2–3 minutes.

Roughly spread the mushroom mixture over the base of the pan and pour over the beaten egg. Swirl the pan around to coat the base with the egg. Leave to set undisturbed on the heat for 1–2 minutes then sprinkle over the Feta cheese. Place the pan under a hot grill for about 1 minute or until the egg is lightly cooked and the Feta cheese just beginning to melt.

Season the omelette with plenty of ground black pepper and parsley and serve immediately.

Try . . .

• Serving the omelettes in salad-filled pitta breads or on toasted slices of black olive ciabatta.

• For a heartier supper, leave the egg quite softly cooked and serve on grilled gammon steaks topped with soured cream.

Simmered Potatoes with Bacon and Garlic
Serves 2

I use less and less cream when cooking now – not for any particular health reasons but mainly because I prefer lighter, fresher
flavours. However, there are times when I feel in need of something rich and mellow and often turn to this creamy potato dish
that's loosely based on the classic Pommes Dauphinoise –
a garlic-scented gratin of potatoes with cream that requires
hours of long, slow baking. It's an all time favourite for me in
spite of the fact that I cooked it every evening for over a year in
the very first restaurant I worked at in the heart of Lancashire.

This faster version simmers the potatoes on the hob with
bacon and crème fraîche until they are melting and tender.
Serve with some roast chicken, crispy-grilled lamb cutlets or
just with a crisp fresh salad on the side. It makes a soothing
supper when all you want to do is curl up on a frosty night.

> 350g/12oz waxy 'salad' potatoes
> olive oil
> 3 fat garlic cloves, peeled and sliced
> a small handful diced smoked bacon or lardons
> 100ml/4fl oz full-fat crème fraîche whisked with enough
>   full-fat milk to give the consistency of single cream
> salt and ground black pepper

Thinly slice the potatoes into rounds no thicker than a pound
coin. There's no need to peel them. Drizzle a little olive oil over
the base of a non-stick frying pan (one suitable for popping under
the grill) and heat until the oil begins to shimmer. Add the garlic
and bacon and fry together for 3–4 minutes until the bacon has
released most of its fat into the pan and is beginning to colour.
Stir in the potatoes and cook for at least 10 minutes, depending
on the thickness of the slices, until they begin to soften.

Season the crème fraîche mixture and pour over the potatoes. Increase the heat until the liquid just starts to bubble then cover the pan with a lid or baking sheet. Turn the heat as low as possible so that the potatoes simmer slowly for a further 5–10 minutes or until they are very soft and tender.

Finish the potatoes under a hot grill for 2–3 minutes until golden brown.

Jerusalem artichokes . . . the knobbly creamy beige tubers that make magical soups are delicious fried or roasted with bacon and they make a good addition to this recipe. Reduce the quantity of potatoes by about 125g/4oz and substitute the same quantity of peeled and sliced artichokes. Cut off the worst knobbles then peel them with a swivel peeler smoothing down any remaining rough edges. Thickly slice the artichokes and mix them with the potatoes. A word of warning – they do discolour quickly so have everything else ready before you start to peel and slice them. Otherwise cover them with cold water and lemon juice to keep them creamy white.

Asparagus with Crispy Bacon and Egg
Serves 2

Asparagus doesn't travel well. No matter how often I'm tempted to buy imported spears from Chile or Spain they just cannot match the taste of English asparagus. At the first sight of the new crop I'm off down to Garson Farm, a haven of pick-your-own produce in Surrey. I don't go as often as I would like to but I couldn't miss their asparagus season.

My favourite snack when I return home from an orgy of picking is usually a soft-boiled egg with asparagus 'soldiers'. And when the supplies of asparagus approach a glut and the price falls, I take two fat bundles of spears and make this supper. It's not quite an omelette as there's more 'filling' than egg and it's not truly a frittata as it's soft and creamy but it is a heavenly combination of salty bacon, asparagus and lightly set egg. I always fill a whole frying pan as any left over is delicious cold (though not straight from the fridge) in a crusty baguette. If you have any summer evening picnics planned it's ideal to take along cut into fat wedges.

Finally, there is a lot of nonsense talked about cooking asparagus and many very expensive pans sold for the purpose. The truth is that it can be treated just like any other green vegetable and simply dropped into a large saucepan of boiling, salted water. Begin testing the stalks with a knife after about 3 minutes; some larger stalks will take 7–10 minutes.

1 bundle asparagus spears, about 450g/1lb
salt and ground black pepper
small knob of butter, preferably unsalted
1 shallot or 1 small onion, finely chopped
1 garlic clove, sliced
3 eggs, beaten together with a tablespoon of water
75g/3oz soft fresh goat's cheese or diced Fontina or
    Mozzarella cheese

50g/2oz smoked streaky bacon, diced
handful fresh basil leaves

Bend the asparagus spears around the middle of the stalk. They
should snap crisply where the tender spear ends and the tougher
stalk begins. Drop the spears into a large saucepan of boiling,
salted water. Return to the boil and begin testing the spears
with the point of a knife after about 3 minutes. Drain the spears
into a colander when they are just tender. Run them under cold
water to stop them cooking any further, then leave them to
drain.

Melt the butter in a large frying pan and fry the shallot with
the garlic over a moderate heat until it turns a rich golden
brown – perhaps a little darker than you might usually cook it.
Tip the shallot into the beaten eggs then season with a little salt
and plenty of pepper. Drop teaspoon sized blobs of the goat's
cheese into the egg or add the diced cheese, but don't stir it in.

Return the frying pan to the heat and add the bacon. Fry
over a high heat until it is golden brown, sizzling and crisp
around the edges.

Lower the heat a little then scatter the asparagus and basil
over the bacon. Give the egg mixture a quick stir and pour it
evenly into the pan.

Leave undisturbed to set for 1–2 minutes then pop the
whole pan under the grill for a further 1–2 minutes to cook the
top. The egg should be just set and creamy, not firm. Eat warm
with crusty bread and perhaps a salad.

For vegetarians . . . omit the bacon and fry double the quantity of
shallots or onion or add some sliced mushrooms.

Baked Tatties with
Finnan Haddie and Chives
Serves 2

When hit by a winter cold or flu, the foods I choose to comfort and soothe are always the same – hot, buttered toast and Marmite, tinned tomato soup and large, floury, baked potatoes. The toast must be thick and the butter unsalted, the soup must be Heinz and the potato not sad and limp from the microwave but a fat Maris Piper or Golden Wonder rubbed with oil and salt then baked till its skin is crisp and cracking, its flesh fluffy, white and steaming.

2 large floury baking potatoes, Golden Wonder, King Edward
    or Maris Piper
olive oil
salt and coarsely ground black pepper
1 medium fillet of finnan haddie (smoked haddock)
large knob of butter
juice of 1 small lemon
about 4 tablespoons crème fraîche (the reduced-fat one is
    fine)
small bunch chives or spring onions, chopped

Scrub the potatoes, rub them all over with olive oil, then salt and pepper. Put them on the bars of a hot oven, 200C/400F/gas mark 6, for about 1 hour, probably a bit longer, depending of course on the size of potato. The skin should be golden and crisp and the flesh very soft.

Cover the smoked haddock with cold water for 10–15 minutes to remove some of its saltiness.

When the potato has been in the oven for a good 30 minutes drain the haddock and put it in a shallow, buttered ovenproof dish. Squeeze over the juice of half a lemon then cover with a piece of buttered foil and pop the fish in the oven alongside the potato for about 10–15 minutes or until it is just cooked. Check for doneness after 10 minutes, the fish should be opaque and the flesh fall into flakes easily.

Remove the potato from the oven and split open lengthways. Scoop the flesh out of the potato skins (easiest done with a spoon) into a bowl and add a good knob of butter, the juices from the baked haddock and the crème fraîche. Mash with a fork until smooth then add the flaked haddock and the chives. Don't be too heavy handed or the haddock will break into little pieces – try to keep it in whole flakes. Taste for seasoning; you might want to add a little more lemon juice if the haddock is very salty.

Spoon the mixture back into the potato skins and pop back into the hot oven for about 10 minutes until the top is beginning to brown. Serve with dollops of chilled crème fraîche on top and a peppery watercress salad.

Tarte Flambé

Serves 2

I can claim no credit for this extraordinarily simple and utterly delicious tart. It is a regional speciality of Alsace which I first tasted years ago in the villages around Strasbourg; a combination of thin crust, creamy onions and crisp bacon. When eaten with a green salad tossed with slightly vinegary vinaigrette it makes one of the tastiest suppers imaginable. I do cheat and use a bread mix for the base but if you have a favourite pizza dough recipe use that. But don't be tempted to use one of the part-baked pizza bases that are available; it just won't be thin and crispy enough. Most of the major supermarkets now stock ready-chopped lardons of Italian pancetta or smoked bacon. These handy little nuggets make this recipe a snip to do but if you can't find them buy streaky bacon as thickly sliced as possible and cut it into dice.

> 280g white bread or pizza base mix
> olive oil
> about 12 shallots, thinly sliced
> 2 garlic cloves, crushed
> 200ml tub crème fraîche
> 200g/7oz lardons Italian pancetta or smoked bacon
> a good handful fresh thyme leaves
> salt and freshly ground black pepper

Tip the bread mix into a large bowl and add the recommended quantity of warm water. Mix together to give a firm but slightly sticky dough, then knead for 5 minutes. If the mixing bowl is large enough I usually just pummel the dough around in it but if you have a mixer with a dough hook, use that instead.

Preheat the oven to its highest setting and put two baking sheets (preferably non-stick) in to heat up.

Turn the dough out, cut it in half and place each half on a sheet of oiled foil. Press each piece with your fist into very thin, rough rounds about 20.5cm/8 inch in diameter.

Put the sliced shallot into a bowl and separate into rings. Add the garlic and crème fraîche; stir until all the shallot is coated with cream then divide the mixture evenly between the two rounds of dough. Scatter the lardons of bacon and thyme leaves over the top then season everything very lightly with salt and generously with black pepper. Leave to rise a little in a warm place for about 15 minutes.

Using a fish slice or spatula to help you, slide the rounds off the foil and onto the hot baking sheets. Drizzle with a little olive oil, then bake at 220C/425F/gas mark 7 for 30 minutes until the bases are crisp and the bacon golden and crispy. If the dough needs a little longer turn the temperature down to 180C/350F/gas mark 4 for a further 10–15 minutes.

Transferring the dough . . . from oiled foil to heated baking sheets may seem a bit of a fiddle but that initial blast of heat does help to cook and crisp the base of the dough.

If the shallots . . . are sliced very thinly they will be cooked and tender in this time but if you prefer you can fry them in a drizzle of oil for 5–7 minutes to soften a little before using. Let them cool before adding to the crème fraîche.

Baked Leeks with Mascarpone and Bacon
Serves 2

This is a slightly updated version of one of my favourite Cordon Bleu classics. When the evenings become longer and colder, I think that it's one of the most comforting suppers in the world and utterly delicious. I love it quite simply with salad and chunks of crusty bread to mop up every bit of the slightly burnt, cheesy sauce. Or, if I remember, I'll rub two large tatties with a little oil and salt and slip them into the oven to start baking about half an hour before cooking the leeks.

> 6 slim leeks, barely thicker than your thumb
> salt and ground black pepper
> 125g/4oz mascarpone cheese or a full fat soft cheese
> small pot single cream
> a teaspoon of English or Dijon mustard
> 50g/2oz mature Cheddar cheese, coarsely grated
> 6 thin rashers rindless streaky bacon or thinly sliced baked
>   ham
> about 25g/1oz good white bread such as ciabatta

Cut any coarse green tops off the leeks then slice them into short finger lengths. Wash them thoroughly under the cold tap to rinse away any grit. Drop the leeks into a large pan of boiling, salted water and leave them to bubble until tender. Depending on their thickness, test the leeks with the point of a sharp knife after 5 minutes. Drain them well. They can hold a surprising amount of water so I usually stand them on end in a colander to drain while I make the sauce.

Put the mascarpone in a bowl and gradually beat in the cream and mustard until the mixture is smooth, then stir in half the grated cheese. Add a good grinding of black pepper (there should be enough salt in the bacon and cheese).

Squeeze the leeks lightly to remove any remaining liquid and put them in a buttered, shallow ovenproof dish. Stretch the bacon rashers with the back of a knife then cut in half. Wrap a piece of bacon or ham loosely around small bundles of leeks. Then spread them out into a single layer in the dish.

Spoon the cream sauce over the leeks – they should be barely covered – then sprinkle over the remaining cheese and the breadcrumbs.

Bake at 190C/375F/gas mark 5 for about 20–25 minutes or until the top is a deep golden brown and beginning to burn at the edges. To speed this up increase the oven temperature to 220C/425F/gas mark 7 for a further 5–10 minutes or pop the dish under a hot grill to toast the top before serving.

Bonfire Supper
Serves 2

This is a great family favourite although not one for every day of the week as it is very rich. With its crispy, golden edges and rich buttery sauce, it's the perfect supper to come home to after an evening round the bonfire.

225g/1lb new potatoes, halved
225g/1lb pumpkin, peeled and thinly sliced
1 large onion, finely sliced
salt and freshly ground black pepper
50g/2oz thinly sliced smoked ham, roughly chopped
125g/4oz buttery cheese, such as Taleggio, Gruyère,
    Emmental or Jarlsberg, sliced
150ml/5fl oz crème fraîche

Preheat the oven to 220C/425F/gas mark 7. Boil the potatoes, pumpkin and onion together in salted water in a shallow, flame-proof casserole for 3–4 minutes only. Drain off all the liquid and mix in the ham and cheese but leave the mixture very rough, this isn't one of those neatly layered gratins.

The crème fraîche is very thick so beat in a little cold water, just enough to bring it to a thick pouring consistency. Season it well with plenty of pepper then pour the cream evenly over the potato mixture. Place the whole dish on the hob and bring to the boil.

Now put the dish in the oven and bake for about 30 minutes or until bubbling and a deep golden brown. As the mixture cooks it forms a golden crust on top. I like to stir this in 2 or 3 times during the cooking time as you would for a rice pudding. Press the tip of a knife down into the centre of one of the potatoes to make sure that they are tender then serve.

If cooked the night before . . . reserve a little of the crème fraîche mixture to brush over the top before reheating the following day in a hot oven for about 15–20 minutes. If the top is very well browned then cover the dish with foil while it heats and bring back the crispy top by putting it under the grill for 2–3 minutes.

For vegetarians . . . omit the ham and use an extra 125g/4oz of potatoes or pumpkin. Sweet potatoes and celeriac are also good to use.

CHAPTER 6

Served with . . .

Sizzling Greens
Serves 2

A pan full of sizzling Chinese greens is the only extra accompaniment you might want some evenings and will take all of two minutes to do. Pak choy is a particular favourite of mine for stir-frying with its plump white stalk and soft green leafy top but there are plenty of Chinese greens to choose from now.

225g/8oz pak choy
1 knob fresh root ginger
1 or 2 garlic cloves
oil
sesame oil

Cut off the leafy tops and tear into bite-size pieces, then roughly shred the white stalks. Peel and thinly slice the ginger and garlic. Warm a little oil in a frying pan or wok and fry the ginger and garlic together until they're just beginning to turn golden. Turn the heat up and add the shredded white stalks. Fry, stirring continuously for 1 minute then add the green leaves. Stir-fry for a further minute until it's all sizzling, then season and drizzle over a few drops of sesame oil before serving immediately.

Butter-baked Squash
Serves 2

Squashes make the easiest of accompaniments. There are so many available now but I have my two favourites – the dark green ridged acorn with its bright orange flesh and the creamy butternut.

> 1 butternut or acorn squash
> a large knob of butter, melted
> pinch of brown sugar and ground cinnamon, optional
> salt and freshly ground black pepper

Quarter the squash (they are all much the same size) and scoop out the seeds. Don't try to peel the squash, it's much too difficult; just place the wedges, skin side down, in a single layer in a roasting tin and brush with melted butter. Try a little sprinkle of brown sugar and ground cinnamon too.

Season with plenty of salt and pepper and cook at 220C/400F/gas mark 7 for about 30 minutes or until tender and lightly browned. Scoop the soft flesh off the skin as you're eating it – or just eat it skin and all as I do.

Fast-fried Broccoli
Serves 2

Broccoli is ideal for stir-frying and rewards you with its glorious vivid green colour and fresh flavour. I tend to buy the slender stems of purple sprouting broccoli that need virtually no trimming and cook in minutes. To cut down on the cooking time thinly slice the broccoli right through from head to stalk.

350g/12oz broccoli, sliced
oil
½ red chilli, de-seeded and chopped
salt and freshly ground black pepper
lemon juice

Heat a little oil in a large frying pan or wok and stir in the broccoli with the chopped red chilli. Toss everything over a medium heat for about 5–7 minutes or until the heads are tender then splash about 6 tablespoonfuls of cold water into the hot pan. Cover with a lid or baking sheet and leave the broccoli to steam for 2–3 minutes. Season generously with salt, pepper and a squeeze of lemon juice, then serve.

Celeriac Mash
Serves 2

I love to mix potatoes with the mild celery flavour of celeriac –
the combination makes a great partner for beef and pork. I prefer
to leave the mash quite rough with chunks of celeriac peppered
through the potato.

> 450g/1lb potatoes (Maris Piper, Desirée or King Edwards),
>   peeled and roughly chopped
> 225g/8oz celeriac, peeled and chopped
> salt and freshly ground black pepper
> juice of half a lemon
> butter

Put the vegetables in a pan of cold, salted water with the lemon
juice to stop the celeriac discolouring. Bring to the boil and
cook until both are quite soft. Drain the vegetables and return
to the pan.

Shake them over a low heat to dry off any moisture, then
mash with plenty of butter and seasoning.

Baked Carrots with Saffron and Orange
Serves 2

225g/8oz carrots, peeled and cut into thick fingers
few strands saffron
1 handful fresh thyme leaves
a large knob of butter
finely grated rind and juice of 1 small orange
salt and freshly ground black pepper

Preheat the oven to 220C/425F/gas mark 7. Lay a large double thickness of foil on the work surface and put the carrots in the centre with all the other ingredients except the orange juice. Bring the sides of the foil up and scrunch together to form a 'bag'. Pour in the orange juice and seal the top. Bake in the oven for 35–40 minutes or until just tender.

Glazed Beetroot with Herb
and Garlic Vinaigrette
Serves 2

225g/8oz small raw baby beetroot
2 fat garlic cloves, crushed
a small handful fresh oregano, roughly chopped
salt and freshly ground black pepper
50ml/2fl oz balsamic vinegar
50ml/2fl oz extra virgin olive oil
1 tablespoon redcurrant jelly

Preheat the oven to 200C/400F/gas mark 6. Lay a large double thickness of foil on the work surface and put the beetroot in the centre. Put all the other ingredients in a small saucepan and warm together until the redcurrant jelly melts. Taste for seasoning. Bring the sides of the foil up and scrunch together to form a 'bag'. Pour in the warm 'vinaigrette' and seal the top. Bake in the oven for about 1½ hours or until just tender.

Salt and Pepper Crusted Potatoes
Serves 2

These tiny roasted potatoes are unbelievably succulent and tasty, just as irresistible as chips but a bit healthier.

450g/1lb new potatoes, rinsed or wiped
2 tablespoons olive oil
1 tablespoon each of sea salt and coarsely ground black pepper

Preheat oven to 220C/425F/gas mark 7. Halve any large potatoes. They should be big enough for just one or two mouthfuls. Put the potatoes in an even layer in a roasting tin, drizzle over the oil and sprinkle with the salt and pepper. Shake the pan to make sure all the potatoes are coated with oil and seasoning.

Put the tin in the oven and roast the potatoes for about 20–25 minutes or until they are golden brown and tender to the point of a knife. Shake the tin once or twice during cooking to brown the potatoes evenly. Serve immediately or turn the oven down to 170C/325F/gas mark 3 and keep warm for up to 30 minutes.

Mashed Roasted Parsnips with Rosemary and Orange
Serves 2

Roasted with rosemary and mashed with orange, these parsnips are the perfect partner for roast pork, gammon or simply sausages. If you want to cut down on fat then simply boil the parsnips with the rosemary sprigs until very tender. Drain and mash with butter and orange rind as below.

    450g/1lb parsnips, peeled
    salt and freshly ground black pepper
    2 tablespoons sunflower or corn oil
    1 sprig fresh rosemary
    a large knob of butter
    grated rind of 1 orange and a squeeze of juice

Preheat the oven to 200C/400F/gas mark 6. Cut the parsnips into even-sized pieces and boil in salted water for 1 minute. Heat the oil in a large roasting tin. Drain the parsnips well and stir into the hot oil with the rosemary sprigs. Roast for 30–35 minutes or until golden brown and very tender.

Remove the rosemary and roughly mash the parsnips with the butter, orange rind and a little juice. Season well.

Spinach and Watercress Salad
Serves 2

2 handfuls washed young spinach leaves or gem lettuce
1 bunch watercress
about 1 tablespoon chopped flat-leaf parsley
4–5 tablespoons olive oil
1 tablespoon red wine vinegar
salt and freshly ground black pepper

Throw the spinach, watercress and parsley into a salad bowl. Whisk the oil and vinegar together and season to taste with salt and pepper. Toss gently through the leaves and serve immediately.

Soft Leaf Salad
Serves 2

1 plump garlic clove
salt and ground black pepper
4 teaspoons white wine vinegar
6 tablespoons good olive oil
½ teaspoon mustard, English or Dijon
about 3 handfuls of gem lettuce leaves

Whisk together all the dressing ingredients and toss through the leaves. Eat immediately.

Steamed Couscous

Serves 2

175g/6oz couscous
a large knob of butter
1 large red chilli, de-seeded
small handful of toasted blanched almonds
small handful of golden raisins
2 tablespoons chopped fresh parsley
3 tablespoons chopped fresh mint
salt and ground black pepper

Put the couscous in a bowl and pour over about 150ml/5fl oz water or stock. Leave to soak for about 15 minutes, by which time the couscous will have absorbed most of the liquid. Break up the lumps that form with your fingers.

Melt the butter in a large non-stick frying pan and fry the couscous with the chilli, almonds and raisins for 3–4 minutes or until warm. Stir the herbs in with a fork to fluff up the grains and season well. Serve straight away. Remember to remove the chilli if using to avoid any accidents.

Basmati Rice

Serves 2

This is the best method I've tried of cooking basmati rice. It gives dry fluffy grains every time. I have friends who swear by the microwave but I can never seem to get it quite right.

1 cupful white basmati rice
a teaspoon salt

Put the rice in a saucepan with a tight-fitting lid. Add 1 cupful cold water and top up if necessary until the level of water comes to about 2.5cm/1 inch above the level of the grains.

Cover the pan and bring to the boil. Bubble for 1 minute, then reduce the heat to a simmer for another 10 minutes. Turn off the heat and leave the rice (still covered) for 5 minutes. Lift the lid, fluff up the grains with a fork and spoon the rice onto hot plates straight away.

Index

INDEX

Asparagus:
  Asparagus with Crispy Bacon
    and Egg, 168
Aubergine:
  Aubergine, Pepper and Basil
    Parmigiana, 156
  Spiced Aubergine and Sweet
    Potato Stew, 154

Bacon:
  Asparagus with Crispy Bacon
    and Egg, 168
  Baked Leeks with Mascarpone
    and Bacon, 174
  Crumbed Mackerel with
    Crispy Bacon, 13
  Grilled Gammon with Spice
    Rub and Mango Mojo, 76
  Mushroom and Pancetta
    Linguine, 144
  Simmered Potatoes with
    Bacon and Garlic, 166
  Spaghetti with Toasted Walnuts
    and Smoky Bacon Sauce,
    142
  Tarte Flambé, 172
Basmati Rice, 192
Beef:
  Oxtail for a Cold January Day,
    104
  Pan-fried Steak, 94

Saturday Night Supper, 100
Slow-cooked Oxtail with
    Pepper, Thyme and Orange,
    102
Steak with Sugared Onions,
    Mustard and Beer, 98
Stovies, 106
Summer Meat Loaf with
    Roasted Peppers and Garlic,
    108
Beetroot:
  Glazed Beetroot with Herb
    and Garlic Vinaigrette,
    186
Bonfire Supper, 176
Broccoli:
  Fast-fried Broccoli, 183

Carrots:
  Baked Carrots with Saffron
    and Orange, 185
Celeriac:
  Celeriac Mash, 184
Cheese:
  Baked Leeks with Mascarpone
    and Bacon, 174
  Bonfire Supper, 176
  Garlic and Parmesan Risotto,
    136
  Gnocchi with Buttered Leeks
    and Gruyère, 126

Mushroom and Feta Omelette, 164

Noodles with Hot Ham and Parmesan Cream, 145

Pork Escalopes with a Goat's Cheese Crust, 66

Risotto with Two Cheeses, 124

Slow-cooked Onions with Melting Cheese, 162

Three Cheese Macaroni, 130

Chicken and Game:

Chicken, Bean and Spinach Curry, 41

Chicken Escalopes Parmigiana, 58

Coconut and Coriander Chicken, 54

Grilled Lemon and Ginger Chicken, 38

Lemon and Sesame Chicken, 31

Monday Night Risotto, 138

Mustard and Basil Chicken, 32

Oven-baked Chicken with Rosemary and Cracked Garlic, 56

Roast Chicken with a Devilled Sauce, 57

Roast Chicken with Garlic and Wine, 36

Roast Chicken with Honey Dressing, 51

Roast Pheasant with Orange and Juniper, 42

Slow-simmered Chicken with Apple and Lentils, 46

Spiced Saffron Chicken and Figs, 48

Sticky Chicken, 34

Tray-baked Chicken and Artichoke Supper, 44

Chicken Liver:

Pasta with Chicken Liver, Sausage and Chilli Sauce, 132

Coconut:

Coconut and Coriander Chicken, 54

Coconut Fish Curry, 28

Couscous:

Minted Couscous, 50

Steamed Couscous, 191

Duck:

Crispy Duck with Hot Sweet Dip, 52

Eggs:

Asparagus with Crispy Bacon and Egg, 168

Baked Eggs on Roasted Pepper 'Stew', 151

Mushroom and Feta Omelette, 164

Fish and Shellfish:

Baked Plaice with Polenta Crumbs, 26

Baked Tatties with Finnan Haddie and Chives, 170

Chilli Noodles and Prawns, 139

Coconut Fish Curry, 28

Crumbed Mackerel with Crispy Bacon, 13

Grilled Salmon with Lemon and Caper Butter Sauce, 18

Fish and Shellfish (*continued*)
  Mussels in Cider and Saffron
    Broth, 16
  Quick Fish Pie, 6
  Roast Cod with Lime and
    Chilli, 4
  Roasted Fish with Warm
    Potato and Tarragon Salad,
    14
  Salmon in a Puff of Pastry, 24
  Salmon Roasted with a Spiced
    Crumb Crust, 8
  Salt-baked Trout, 20
  Scallops with Sweet Chilli
    Sauce, 22
  Skate with Hot Tomato Salsa, 3
  Thai Prawn Cakes, 10

Garlic:
  Garlic and Parmesan Risotto,
    136
  Glazed Beetroot with Herb
    and Garlic Vinaigrette, 186
  Oven-baked Chicken with
    Rosemary and Cracked
    Garlic, 56
  Roast Chicken with Garlic
    and Wine, 36
  Simmered Potatoes with
    Bacon and Garlic, 166
  Spaghetti with Crispy Garlic
    Crumbs, 121
  Summer Meat Loaf with
    Roasted Peppers and Garlic,
    108
Gnocchi:
  Gnocchi with Buttered Leeks
    and Gruyère, 126
  Gnocchi Puttanesca, 140

Green Tomato and Mayonnaise
    Tart, 160

Lamb:
  Braised Lamb Shanks with
    Harissa, 74
  Butterfly Lamb with Onion
    and Cumin, 78
  Grilled Lamb with Lemon and
    Melting Onions, 72
  Herby Lamb with Avocado
    Hummous, 90
  Lamb and Rosemary Ragu,
    146
  Red Lamb and Pumpkin
    Coconut Curry, 80
  Roast Rack of Lamb with
    Yoghurt and Spices, 84
  Slow-cooked Lamb with
    Oranges and Sherry
    Vinegar, 88
Leeks:
  Baked Leeks with Mascarpone
    and Bacon, 174
  Gnocchi with Buttered Leeks
    and Gruyère, 126
  Leek and Mustard Butter
    Sauce, 96
Liver:
  Pan-fried Liver with Marsala
    and Onions, 92

Mango:
  Mango with Lime and Chilli,
    40
  Mango and Mint Relish,
    86
Meatballs with Olive and Pesto
    Pasta, 134

Mushrooms:
Mushroom and Feta Omelette, 164
Mushroom and Pancetta Linguine, 144

Onions:
Butterfly Lamb with Onion and Cumin, 78
Grilled Lamb with Lemon and Melting Onions, 72
Onion and Red Wine Gravy, 112
Pan-fried Liver with Marsala and Onions, 92
Slow-cooked Onions with Melting Cheese, 162
Soured Cream and Caramelized Onion Tarts, 152
Steak with Sugared Onions, Mustard and Beer, 98

Parsnips:
Mashed Roasted Parsnips with Rosemary and Orange, 188
Pasta and Noodles:
Chilli Noodles and Prawns, 139
Gnocchi with Buttered Leeks and Gruyère, 126
Gnocchi Puttanesca, 140
Lamb and Rosemary Ragu, 146
Meatballs with Olive and Pesto Pasta, 134
Mushroom and Pancetta Linguine, 144

Noodles with Hot Ham and Parmesan Cream, 145
Pappardelle with Sausage, Rosemary and Red Wine, 122
Pasta with Chicken Liver, Sausage and Chilli Sauce, 132
Pasta with Pesto and Fresh Peas, 128
Spaghetti with Crispy Garlic Crumbs, 121
Spaghetti with Toasted Walnuts and Smoky Bacon Sauce, 142
Stir-fried Pork with Cappelletti and Mustard, 143
Three Cheese Macaroni, 130
Pastries:
Green Tomato and Mayonnaise Tart, 160
Salmon in a Puff of Pastry, 24
Soured Cream and Caramelized Onion Tarts, 152
Tarte Flambé, 172
Pheasant:
Roast Pheasant with Orange and Juniper, 42
Pork:
Hoisin and Honey Ribs, 63
Pork Chops with Apple and Fennel, 64
Pork Chops with Fresh Plums and Ginger, 68
Pork Escalopes with a Goat's Cheese Crust, 66

Pork (*continued*)
Pork Steaks with Sage and
Apple, 70
Shredded Pork Wraps, 82
Stir-fried Pork with Cappelletti
and Mustard, 143
Summer Meat Loaf with
Roasted Peppers and Garlic,
108
Potatoes:
Baked Tatties with Finnan
Haddie and Chives, 170
Bonfire Supper, 176
Roasted Fish with Warm
Potato and Tarragon Salad,
14
Salt and Pepper Crusted
Potatoes, 187
Simmered Potatoes with
Bacon and Garlic, 166

Rice:
Garlic and Parmesan Risotto,
136
Monday Night Risotto, 138
Risotto with Two Cheeses, 124

Salad:
Soft Leaf Salad, 190
Spinach and Watercress Salad,
189
Sauces, Dips and Dunks:
Crème Fraîche and
Horseradish Sauce, 21
Fresh Tomato and Chilli Sauce,
27
Hot Sweet Dip, 53
Leek and Mustard Butter
Sauce, 96

Mango with Lime and Chilli,
40
Mango and Mint Relish,
86
Onion and Red Wine Gravy,
112
Simple Tomato Sauce, 158
Sweet and Sour Coriander
Dressing, 12
Sausages:
Meatballs with Olive and Pesto
Pasta, 134
Oven-baked Sausage and Bean
Pot, 114
Pappardelle with Sausage,
Rosemary and Red
Wine, 122
Pasta with Chicken Liver,
Sausage and Chilli Sauce,
132
Sausages in Red Onion
Marmalade, 113
Toad-in-the-Hole, 110
Venison Sausages with Lentils
and Red Wine, 116
Shortcut Shortcrust, 159
Sizzling Greens, 181
Squash:
Butter-baked Squash, 182
Stovies, 106
Summer Meat Loaf with Roasted
Peppers and Garlic, 108

Tarte Flambé, 172
Thai Prawn Cakes, 10
Thai Red Curry Paste, 87

Vegetables *see* asparagus, aubergine
etc.